The Biggest Lie Ever Told
Fourth Edition

By Malik H. Jabbar

Published By

Rare Books Distributor
P. O. Box 3224
Dayton, Ohio 45401

http://www.TheChristMyth.com

A Treatise On Comparative Religion

i

The Biggest Lie Ever Told, 4th Edition

THE BIGGEST LIE EVER TOLD

FOURTH EDITION

Third Printing 2012

LIBRARY OF CONGRESS CATALOG CARD NUMBER

2006907490

ISBN 10: 1-57154-007-5

ISBN 13: 978-1-57154-007-2

A Treatise On Comparative Religion

The Biggest Lie Ever Told, 4th Edition

PREFACE

This is the fourth edition of this book "The Biggest Lie Ever Told". The book has been extensively revised and enhanced. This edition of the book contains more than twice the content of the previous volume. Much of the commentary has been diligently refined pursuant to greater clarity. We have also added a great deal of information relevant to religious esotericism and mythology that was not included in the previous volumes.

The purpose of this book is to serve as a primer for those entering into the arena of *Secular Theological Research*; and what is Secular Theological Research – it is research based on reason and facts, governed by scientific methods of investigation, and not influenced by popular opinions or favored dogmas. Secular Theologists are not guided by faith in any particular creed, but rather follow paths charted by reason and pragmatism. They are investigators first and believers or nonbelievers second, depending on the prevailing winds of reasonable evidences or lack thereof. Secular Theologists do not accept the concepts of so-called godly revelations, or sacred scriptures – to do so would be tantamount to exempting said sacred scriptures from our critical examinations, because such documents (scriptures) would be deemed inviolable by reason of their so-called sacred sources; therefore the word "sacred" does not exist in the working vocabulary of Secular Theologists. All scriptures from all religions are viewed with equal skepticism, and are judged worthy or unworthy solely as dictated by the yardsticks of truth; and truth, as you know, tends to be reasonable, logical, plausible, and oftentimes verifiable when researched.

This book contains all the information that was listed in the previous volume, plus much more, as I have indicated above. The interconnections between religion and mythology are explored extensively; also the various cultural and earthly environmental affects that influenced mankind's attitudes or conceptions of god are examined in vivid detail.

A Treatise On Comparative Religion

The Biggest Lie Ever Told, 4th Edition

In reference to the Precessional cycles of 25,920 years and the recurring Glacial Epochs – subjects which were touched upon in the previous editions, evidence is intriguing that the intervals between Glacial Epochs had been calculated by the Ancients. The descent of the glaciers from the Polar Regions is a phenomenon that occurs at regular defined intervals is the indication. Of course when this occurs, the impact upon the inhabitants of this planet is devastating. If this premise is correct, it adds further understanding to the importance of correct Time tracking, as it relates to Astrological cycles of 2160 years, the Great Year of 25920 years and to other cycles of much greater duration, which are reviewed in another essay.

Today, in this Inter-Glacial era, glaciers cover over 10% of the earth's land surface. The scientist (geologists) tell us that there are mountains of ice lodged in the Arctic Regions, so much so that if it were free to roam, it would encase our entire planet in a sheet of ice 100 to 200 ft. thick. About 15,000 years ago, the earth was in the last stages of the Ice Age; and over 30% of our planets land surface was encased in Ice. Glaciers, over a mile high in places! All of Ireland was covered, 90% of England; all of Norway, Sweden, Finland, Denmark, vast portions of Russia, Poland, Germany, the Netherlands, Belgium and parts of France were covered by one contiguous solid sheet of ice, thousands of feet thick in places. In North America, one solid sheet of ice covered the entire area from the Polar region as far south as Ohio and Missouri. And, from these immense sheets of ice, covering Europe, Asia and the Americas, huge glaciers broke off, and descended even further south as far as 30 degrees North Latitude.

The effect of the Ice Age on our planet was incalculable, only estimable. It changed the actual contour of our earth; its geography, the earth's crust. The rivers, seas, and oceans - all were changed by the effects of the Ice age. The climate was altered, precipitation ratios were changed, valleys were carved through mountains, deserts and rivers became lakes; the boundaries of the continents were effected as well as the sea levels.

The Biggest Lie Ever Told, 4th Edition

The paragraphs above are a description of our planet during the Ice Age. Our planet is very different today, because we now are living in an Inter-Glacial period, after the Ice Age, after the retreat of the huge masses of ice back to the Polar Regions.

Some believe that the sun in its orbit within the galaxy passes through a hostile region of space that adversely affects the normalcy of our climate. Others believe that the shifting of the points of the Perihelion and Aphelion that cycles at intervals of 21,000 years is a contributor to significant changes in our climate at predictable intervals over thousands of years. Still, others believe that the gradual shifting or sudden shifting of the earths' axis is the culprit or that the eccentricity of the earth's orbit is not constant, but subject to significant variations; also, the fact that the obliquity of the ecliptic is changing in a cycle of millions of years - this factor also must be considered, perhaps preeminently considered. I have given detailed explanations of these cycles in my book, titled "The Lifting Of The Gnostic Veil".

But the fact remains that even though humans have occupied this planet for untold millions of years, and scientists teach us that our planet is over five billion years old, our view of history becomes very murky at about 10,000 years. Could it be that this bountiful planet is periodically transformed into Valley of Death. Is our environment subject to such horrific and devastating variations, so much so that its effect is the periodic destruction of human civilization, and in consequence of this, the Arresting and Restarting of civilization is an eternal recurring process; and did the Ancients successfully calculate the intervals between these destructions and bequeath this knowledge to their progeny under the veil of myth and fable. The evidence is intriguing.

A Treatise On Comparative Religion

TABLE OF CONTENTS

TABLE OF CONTENTS

A Treatise On Comparative Religion

The Biggest Lie Ever Told, 4th Edition

Chapter One: The Nature Of God

The most important questions that confront all of us who study religion are: *What are the true sources of our religious concepts? Are our cultural beliefs derived from god or from man?* If god is the author of monotheism, and if god actually missioned the so-called prophets with this doctrine of monotheism as taught by the Jews, Christians, and Muslims, then our fates are hopelessly sealed, we can only bow down in submission to the Rabbis, Priests, and Imams; await our morbid destinies, and kiss free-will, intellect and reason goodbye – because human rationality and *Free Thought* have no place in a world ruled by so-called regents of god. And I suggest to you that there is no worse hell than living under a system of government controlled by religious zealots. When religionists have the power to impose the rules of the Synagogue, Church, and Mosque into our daily lives, economics, and personal relationships, the result is hell on earth; just think about it! In fact there is an ancient philosophical wisdom that suggests that the earth is, in fact, hell. There were those of old who suggested that the Garden Of Eden was not actually an earthly location, but rather a heavenly domain, ethereal, of the spirits; it was our souls' domain and not of this material world. They teach that our (souls') rebellion or disobedience in the Garden was in the spirit, and our punishment was the sentencing to death, *death in matter*, that our condition of life on this planet is the death sentence that god warned Adam of in the bible; that this planet is actually hell, and our toils and sufferings are the wages of our sins that we committed in heaven, *when in our prior spiritual existences.* This concept is actually confirmed in the Quran of the Muslims: Witness quote from Sura 2, Verses 35-36: "³⁵We said: *O Adam! Dwell thou and thy wife in the Garden; and eat of the bountiful things therein as ye will; but approach not this tree, or ye run into harm and transgression* ³⁶*Then did Satan make them slip from the (garden), and get them out of the state (of felicity) in which they had been. We said: "Get ye down, all (ye people), with enmity between yourselves. On earth will be your dwelling-place and your means of livelihood - for a time."* The preceding Quranic verses clearly depict the Garden of Eden as celestial, and not terrestrial, and the terrestrial earth is indicated as a place of exile. This is in-keeping with the higher wisdom that is known by the enlightened Jews (of the sacerdotal classes) and some others of diverse cultural persuasions, but is grossly misunderstood by most Christian scholars; this knowledge is also accessible in Platonic teachings.

We (souls), according to this philosophy, are now prisoners of hell; our physical bodies are jails or tombs that encase our souls, and the deaths of our material *mortal* bodies are actually opportunities for our *immortal* souls to escape this earthly grave, *to be born again*, i.e. rebirth of the souls, to make their ways back to heaven, paradise, the Garden Of Eden, if we pass successfully through the halls of judgment. **Found also,** in this mix, is the genesis of the concepts of *reincarnation,* and *hell,* concocted explanations for the transitions of the souls that fail the tests of re-entry into heaven, from which we all, allegedly, have been exiled as punishment. The souls that fail to earn their passage back to heaven are continually reincarnated into other bodies as further punishment or straightening for their sins, or under the monotheistic doctrines are sent to eternal damnation into the pits of hell. These reincarnations are alleged to go on indefinitely, or until the aspirants qualify for re-entry into heaven. Aspects of this are, of course, taught within the monotheistic doctrines, and some other *eastern* doctrines, in a confused and convoluted way; actually *they all have profaned the true essence of the truth, as I have come to understand it*. Reincarnation is not normally associated with monotheism, but nevertheless, the *eastern* concepts of potentially indefinite reincarnations of wayward souls, along with the Christian, Islamic concepts of potentially eternal damnation in their assorted hells, were *fabricated* by the priesthoods for the same purposes: that is to provide explanations for the disposition of those souls that did not qualify for re-entry into heaven. The monotheists explain the fate of unpurified souls as being destined for eternal punishment in hell, whereas the Hindus and some others explain this fate as indefinite reincarnations until purification is attained. The stimulus for both concepts (hell and reincarnation) is identical, i.e. an explanation for the transitions of those immortal souls that are not accepted for entry into heaven, and the imposing of religious incentives and warnings upon the believers of the various doctrines. The diverse priesthoods have chosen different paths to explain the transition, but all achieved the same net result of providing their flocks with some acceptable rationale for the alternate destinations of faithful or unfaithful souls, and the fate of the believers are in consequence linked also with their dutiful adherence to their religious creeds. **Christians and Muslims are further deluded** in their concepts of heaven, as a place where believers are reunited with their love ones. We've all heard *believers* talk about how they expect to see their lost loves and families when they pass to the other side; these vain hopes are not even biblical! Note the words of Jesus in the bible when the question was posed to him about family make-up in heaven:

Matthew 22:23 through Matthew 22:30

²³The same day came to him the <u>Sadducees, which say that there is no resurrection,</u> and asked him, ²⁴Saying, Master, Moses said, If a man die, having no children, his brother shall marry his wife, and raise up seed unto his brother. ²⁵Now there were with us seven brethren: and the first, when he had married a wife, deceased, and, having no issue, left his wife unto his brother: ²⁶Likewise the second also, and the third, unto the seventh. ²⁷And last of all the woman died also. ²⁸Therefore in the resurrection whose wife shall she be of the seven? for they all had her. ²⁹Jesus answered and said unto them, Ye do err, not knowing the scriptures, nor the power of God. ³⁰For in the resurrection they neither marry, nor are given in marriage, but are as the angels of God in heaven.

So, according to these verses, regular family bonds do not exist in heaven, rather all members (souls) are wedded to god, and I might add, *for eternity* – that means a billion million years *plus* and no way out! This sounds so ridiculous to me.

But I digress; this is not our focus at this time – the subject of this chapter is the *nature (character) of god*. I have explained the original genesis of these concepts concerning our alleged *fall from heaven*, as well as what I see as errors and misconceptions of the proponents of this doctrine, in my book "The Lifting Of The Gnostic Veil".

Is the author of religion god or man?

This question needs to be carefully pondered, that is the question concerning the true source of our religious concepts – were these confusing, contradictory, and inane concepts truly revealed by god or were these ideas conjured up from within the monasteries and inner sanctums of the sacerdotal assemblies? If the monotheistic doctrines are truly revelations to humanity from the Creator-god, then all that we as humans have to look for, from here to eternity, is contained within the scriptures of the Jews, Christians, and Muslims. Just a couple of the unfortunate consequences of living under a theocratic government, as portrayed in the bible, would be that the system promotes slavery, and women are considered inferior beings; **note god's words**, according to the bible:

Leviticus, Chapter 25, verses 44 to 46:
44. Both thy bondmen, and thy bondmaids, which thou shalt have, shall be of the heathen that are round about you; of them shall ye buy bondmen and bondmaids.
45. Moreover, of the children of the strangers that do sojourn among you, of them shall ye buy, and of their families that are with you, which they begat in your land: and they shall be your possession.
46. And ye shall take them as an inheritance for your children after you, to inherit them for a possession; they shall be your bondmen for ever: but over your brethren the children of Israel, ye shall not rule one over another with rigor.

Timothy, Chapter 6, verse 1:
1. Let as many servants as are under the yoke count their own masters worthy of all honour, that the name of God and his doctrine be not blasphemed.

1 Timothy 2:11 through 1 Timothy 2:14
[11]Let the woman learn in silence with all subjection. [12]But I suffer not a woman to

teach, nor to usurp authority over the man, but to be in silence. ¹³For Adam was first formed, then Eve. ¹⁴And Adam was not deceived, but the woman being deceived was in the transgression.

We must also note that the monotheistic deity is very inefficient. On various occasions, he has destroyed the world, or cities, or regions as punishment, pursuant to the establishment of a better world where the inhabitants live in submission to his edicts. We must remember that allegedly god destroyed the world in the time of Noah because of the sins of the people. His goal, according to the bible and Quran, was to repopulate the planet with communities that would obey his decrees; however, we must conclude that his gambit was a complete failure, because if anything, sin in the world has *increased* since the times of Noah, according to our recorded historical comparisons. He allegedly sent Jesus as a sacrifice for the world's sins, but the world remains unimproved since the times of Jesus – our sins have multiplied, not decreased, so where is the logic in Christ dying for our sins? **As I have noted before, Christ dying for our sins is simply a transference of the Jewish animal sacrifice to human form**, whereas Jesus becomes the sacrificial lamb that serves for an expiation of sins – a pagan sacrificial process that historically crosses almost all ancient cultures, if not, in fact all. The ancient animal or human sacrifice to the gods as an offering or expiation of the sins of the populace or to ward off god's anger is literally everywhere that you look in history (i.e. practiced in every ancient culture)– it amazes me that Christians think the sacrificial concept as it pertains to Jesus is unique. The pagan origin of this primitive concept is so abundantly clear in our world's history that it just bewilders me beyond words that Christian people in general don't recognize the truth of it. The Hebrew sacrifice of the goat or lamb (Jesus) as a scapegoat for the sins of the people is clearly noted in the bible:

Leviticus 16:8
⁸And Aaron shall cast lots upon the two goats; one lot for the LORD, and the other lot for the scapegoat. Leviticus 16:9
⁹And Aaron shall bring the goat upon which the LORD'S lot fell, and offer him for a sin offering. Leviticus 16:15
¹⁵Then shall he kill the goat of the sin offering, that is for the people, and bring his blood within the veil...Leviticus 16:16
¹⁶And he shall make an atonement for the holy place, because of the uncleanness of the children of Israel, and because of their transgressions in all their sins: and so

shall he do for the tabernacle of the congregation, that remaineth among them in the midst of their uncleanness.

So Jesus was a scapegoat just like the animals of the Jewish sacrifices were scapegoats that allegedly expiated the sins of the populace; the only difference is that Jesus is pictured as human instead of animal. The Hebrew-Christians of the incipient Pisces era kept the same Jewish sacrificial theme 99 % intact – they only changed the animal symbol into a human symbol called the Christ, and they declared that Christ was sacrificed for the sins of the entire world, not just the Jews.

It can be truly said that no prophets of the Torah, Bible, or Quran, at the completion of their missions, left behind them a world that was better than they found it, over a sustained period of time. All of these abysmal failures at humanities' reformation do not seem representative of godly wisdom in my opinion. Also, if monotheism was bequeathed to us by the Creator-god, we must also conclude that the creator knows very little about his creation; because according to the bible the world is a flat plain at the center of the universe, with all the stars, planets, moon, and sun revolving around it – so if god wrote the Torah, Bible, and Quran, we must change our scientific views about the structure of the universe. The planet earth must be flat cause god cannot be wrong; of course this was the attitude held by the Monotheists for many centuries, so much so that dissenters of this doctrine were imprisoned, excommunicated, tortured, and killed as opponents of the true faith. But the idea that the world was flat, and that the sun, planets, and stars revolved around the earth, just as the moon does, is a clear reflection of the limited astronomical knowledge possessed by the populace of biblical times. I find it interesting that the geographical and astronomical knowledge of the gods of biblical times, as represented in the scriptures, seems to be on a par with the limited environmental knowledge of the general population – it seems that god possessed the same erroneous concepts of the natural order as the intellectually underdeveloped masses; so who wrote the scriptures – god or man!

Our religious beliefs are, for the most part, accidents of birth; that is to say, we didn't intellectually choose our various individual religious persuasions, but rather most of us were born into the faiths that we practice.

The Biggest Lie Ever Told, 4th Edition

We, for the most part, have not critically examined the credos of our various faiths, but rather we have assumed that our faiths are genuine and accurate. Most of us do not have the courage to introspectively examine our own personal religious beliefs; we'd rather live a lie than to face an unpleasant truth; on the other hand, some of us just need help and guidance in working our way through this intricate labyrinth, called religion. I understand the dilemma; I've spent thirty years studying these matters and there have been times that I wished I didn't know what I know - that this religious world is founded on myths and lies touted as actual history, mixed with deceit, illusions, misconceptions, and vain promises of godly redemption that actually have no foundation whatsoever in fact.

Man has misinterpreted the nature of god

The god of monotheism, that is to say the popular fallacious concept of god, was created by the sacerdotal classes of old, and does not exist as fact; the monotheistic god is a concept created, and envisioned by primitive man, searching for reason for his being. The monotheistic god is a patriarchal god, a father figure, an imagined source of being. It is only natural that primordial man imaged god as parental, because they wanted answers as to their origin and purpose. Primitive mankind thought that they were the only intelligent beings in the universe, and they thought that the world was flat – they did not understand gravity and the solar system accurately. The easiest most understandable concept of the universe that they could envision was that the world was flat, and that all of those myriad cosmic lights that seemed to revolve around their land were indeed doing just that, revolving around their location which they believed sat at the center of the universe.

These major environmental misconceptions were the stimulus that pushed early man into further more spiritually debilitating misconceptions concerning the nature of god. I am referring to the misguided notions of ancient humankind that (# 1) man was the only intelligent life in the universe, and (# 2) that this planet was the center of the universe, and that the entire universe revolved around the earth. It was the aforementioned delusions of man concerning his own nature and status in the universe that caused him to misdiagnose the spiritual nature of god, and further to miscalculate his relationship with god. Since man thought that he was the only intelligent life in the universe, he logically concluded that he was the highest most cherished of all creatures in the universe. He surmised that his bond to his god was comparable to the closest of all relationships that he was familiar with, and the most affectionate relationships that mankind was aware of were the bonds between mother and child, i.e. parental bonds – so man consequently conceptualized his god as parental, as the Father, or Mother in some early cultures, and that the bond between the Father and his creation, accordingly, must have been based on love. Ancient man[1] saw himself as the inheritor of god's treasures, hence he thought of himself as the vicegerent of god on earth. We know that the cosmos is populated by billions of planets, stars, and galaxies flying in their orbits, incalculable light years from us, and each other; but the primitive priests and soothsayers of old saw all the heavenly lights as servants of man – placed in the heavens by the father god in order to light the way of man and to provide man with the means to track time. They thought the stars were linked (attached) to the heavenly dome that they imagined enclosed the universe. **I must repeat:** the errors of early mankind in regards to the natural order, or structure of the universe, lead inevitably to grosser errors in man's conceptions of the force (god) that created the universe. Early man thought that the whole universe revolved around him, and was actually created for him, hence he imagined a god of love whose total focus was on him and his wellbeing. Ancient man saw god as his parent; *this is the most important factor* involved in correctly analyzing the evolution of human thought that engendered the idea of god as a loving benefactor. The attitude of the ancients was that their father was a god whose total active focus was on the welfare of his earthly children. This hopeful and desirable, but nevertheless incorrect concept of god parallels 100% the normal relationship between parents and their children. The mirror to the mind of god is his handiwork, his creation, this grand universe. **We are able to surmise and calculate the**

---

[1] Of course I am using the term "man" in its collective context, in reference to mankind or humanity in general

probable essence and character of god by studying his works, nature. Nature reflects the will and attitude of its creator; it can be no other way. But early man misconstrued the structure of nature, and in consequence misconstrued the character of the creator god. So as man advanced intellectually, and spiritually, and cogitated on the "why" of his existence and the whereabouts and identity of his creator, he formulated his notions of god based on mistaken and erroneous perceptions of the natural order, thereby foredooming his derivations at the very inception of his efforts.

All concepts of god are derived from the mind of man, his inspired imagination; and man's mind is inspired and nurtured by its interaction with the environment, created culture, education, and nature. There is no reliable evidence of the creator-god missioning chosen individuals with godly messages of salvation – such claims are totally bogus. The Jews, Christians, and Muslims have all lied in regards to this matter. I am referring to the spiritual founders, sustainers, and leaders of these religions, not to the lost believers that don't know any better. Actually none of the religions mentioned above were founded by any single individuals, that received great godly revelations - all were formed by groups or factions evolved from previous fraternal societies or associations possessed of certain arcane wisdom, according to what I have been told. And furthermore all of these religions were formed in association with the dominant or aspiring political and financial interest of their regions before achieving lasting success or, at the least, somewhere along the way earned the acquiescence of these powers.

All religions and concepts of god were created by the mind of man, and therefore are partially flawed, and in some cases grossly flawed. These attempts at finding god, through ritualized religion, represent humanities' best efforts, though inadequate, at connecting with the spirit (mind) of our creator. They (the priesthood) asserted anciently, to a populace that was mostly illiterate, that their doctrines descended directly from the mouth of god through revelations; this was claimed in order to give their dogmas divine authority and legitimacy, and this deceitful, reprehensible practice is continued by the clergy of our present era.

Nature Of God

Concerning the nature of god, to which this chapter is dedicated to explaining: a loving doting god is most certainly desirable but the facts of nature do not bear out the assumption that our god, the creator, is overflowing with unlimited love for his human flock. These are hard facts that must be written, in this era. Nature, all of nature is a jungle of merciless contention, with all forms of life vying against and feeding upon other forms of life without pity or refrain. This, I contend, is a look into the mind of god, and if not god – whose mind is represented in the system by which nature perpetuates itself?

Doctrine of Original Sin

This conflict of realities created quite a conundrum for the early, emerging monotheists; they somehow had to resolve their concept of a beneficent god with the stark realities of nature's harshness. It didn't mesh that god could be the ever flowing fountain of love and charity for his human flock but yet our lives are endless tracks of toil, struggle, suffering, sickness, and heartbreak from conception to the grave. So how did the priesthood resolve this conflict of realities is our question! Quite cleverly, I might say – they conjured up the concept of Original Sin; by this concept the onus of man's struggles against the unrelenting onslaughts of natural adversity were placed squarely on the shoulders of humanity itself. The assertion of this dogma is that mankind is under divine punishment because of their disobedience to god in the Garden Of Eden while in the initial era of humankind's sojourn on this planet. As the story goes in Genesis of the bible, when humankind was first created, they were granted eternal life, and an existence free of toil or struggle. God laid down certain basic guidelines for his children's conduct, which included the prohibition of partaking of the fruit of a certain tree within the garden. God declared that the punishment for violating this prohibition would be death. Well, eventually, as the story goes, a serpent visited Eve, while Adam was elsewhere, and convinced her that she would enjoy a better life if she ate the forbidden fruit. Eve, in time, assented to the serpent's suggestion, took a bite of the fruit, subsequently shared the fruit with Adam, and consequently her and Adam's lives were changed forever.

Now, when god, belatedly, found out what they had done, he decreed their punishment forthwith, he declared that the serpent would have to crawl on its belly instead of walking upright, and further that all humankind would thenceforth be condemned to lives of struggle and toil. See bible verses that follow that describe god's declarations:

Genesis 3:14 through Genesis 3:17

[14]And the LORD God said unto the serpent, Because thou hast done this, thou art cursed above all cattle, and above every beast of the field; upon thy belly shalt thou go, and dust shalt thou eat all the days of thy life: [15]And I will put enmity between thee and the woman, and between thy seed and her seed; it shall bruise thy head, and thou shalt bruise his heel.

[16]Unto the woman he said, I will greatly multiply thy sorrow and thy conception; in sorrow thou shalt bring forth children; and thy desire shall be to thy husband, and he shall rule over thee.

[17]And unto Adam he said, Because thou hast hearkened unto the voice of thy wife, and hast eaten of the tree, of which I commanded thee, saying, Thou shalt not eat of it: cursed is the ground for thy sake; in sorrow shalt thou eat of it all the days of thy life;

Romans 5:12

[12]Wherefore, as by one man sin entered into the world, and death by sin; and so death passed upon all men, for that all have sinned:

Romans 5:14

[14]Nevertheless death reigned from Adam to Moses, even over them that had not sinned after the similitude of Adam's transgression, who is the figure of him that was to come.

1 Corinthians 15:22

[22]For as in Adam all die, even so in Christ shall all be made alive.

So in the above, we have, expressed biblically, the essence of the doctrine of mankind's fall; the net result of this fall, according to those that support this doctrine, is that we all are born in sin, subject to the consequences thereof. Of course the devil is alleged to be doing his work also, the devil wants us to be miserable, and to defect from god. So supposedly the devil is running amuck in the world doing everything he can to upset god's plan for us, whatever that plan is. For some reason, even though god is all-powerful, he can't dispense of the devil – the devil must have time to do his work, to tempt, and test us. We are taught that some day god and the devil will have a final showdown and Satan will be vanquished and all those that follow Satan will be destroyed with him. And where does this devil come from? Well the devil is alleged to have been a defector, a fallen angel that rebelled against god, and set out to do his own thing – this is all so weird and cockamamie, in my opinion. There is significant symbolism at the core of the doctrine of Original Sin, but the story, to a great extent, is a tale designed to fix and reconcile the confusing discrepancies between the grim circumstances of human life and a creator god alleged to be the epitome of love, charity, and devotion. The method of the priesthood incorporates the *big promise*, which is the promise that some day, in another realm, our earthly sufferings will end and utopian bliss with god will reign. Of course these promises will never come to fruition in this lifetime or any other lifetime, and once we are dead, it doesn't matter anyway; but the priesthood, along with the politicians, and financiers will take pride in having completed their mission of engendering a citizenry that is stable, patriotic, submissive, and culturally united. And as the duped faithful go to their graves with sincere hopes and faith in fabled heavenly promises that will never ring true, the same lies and falsehoods that worked on them are promulgated to the children of tomorrow as they crawl from their cradles.

God's Law: Survival of the Fittest

But what is the true nature of god – Witness the following quotes from another one of my books "The Lifting Of The Gnostic Veil":
" *It's very jolting and discomforting for most of us to confront the realities of the true character of god, as a dispassionate taskmaster. This goes against the prevailing attitudes of most cultures, that wish to see themselves favored in the eyes of god as most of us are favored in our own eyes.... god (nature) demands efficiency and, in consequence, rewards efficiency when it is achieved; this is god's way and the best way, in my opinion. Nature rewards efficiency, when coupled with wisdom, without fail. The response of nature is*

completely predictable to any set of circumstances if we have the knowledge and wisdom to correctly analyze the situation. The wealth, opulence and convenience that pervades the lives of many in this modern world, as opposed to the pervasive poverty, toil and misery of ages gone by, is clear and indisputable evidence that nature (god) rewards efficiency. Our improved efficiency, in this modern age, has produced greater economic and other associated rewards for us, without doubt. Life is cause and effect and greater efficiency produces greater more favorable effects (results) in whatever endeavors we pursue.

In accordance with god's design, we live in a world of rewards (blessings) and consequences (punishments) which are determined by our causal efforts, coupled with the applications of efficiency and wisdom, in association with good or bad fortune, which is not under our control and may, at times, help or hinder our efforts. Those who are wise, strong, and efficient thrive in a godly world of just rewards and consequences but the weak and inefficient are pulled under, in accordance with god's design....

The concept of a personal god, analogous to parents caring for their children, was clearly designed to instruct people whose intellect was underdeveloped and in the embryonic stages of societal development, with little scientific understanding of the natural environment. Reference this quote from the book Moral And Dogmas by Albert Pike, wherein he quotes a Greek philosopher of the ancient world: "All virtue is a struggle; life is not a scene of repose; but of energetic action. Suffering is but another name for the teaching of experience, appointed by Zeus himself, the giver of all understanding, to be the parent of instruction, the schoolmaster of life. He indeed put an end to the golden age; he gave venom to serpents and predacity to wolves; he shook the honey from the leaf, and stopped the flow of wine in the rivulets; he concealed the element of fire, and made the means of life scanty and precarious. But in all this his object was beneficent; it was not to destroy life, but to improve it. It was a blessing to man, not a curse, to be sentenced to earn his bread by the sweat of his brow; for nothing great or excellent is attainable without exertion; safe and easy virtues are prized neither by gods nor men; and the parsimoniousness of nature is justified by its powerful effect in rousing the dormant faculties, and forcing on mankind the invention of useful arts by means of meditation and thought." This says it all."

The testimony propounded by nature is that god is pure intelligence or ***directive soul (spirit),*** resident in all its creation, animate and inanimate, and it/he functions, punishes and rewards, based on the eternal paradigm of highest reward to the most efficient while the least efficient are subject to attrition. Darwin and others called these natural phenomena the law of the *Survival Of The Fittest*, and there is no better terminology that I am aware of that better describes the judgmental character of god. Mankind imagines a god that is subject to personal request, and favors, a god that punishes him when he errs morally and rewards him when he is pleasing. When examined psychologically as to cause and source, it is easily recognized that this idealized conception of god is, in fact, a transference or attachment of the most exemplary parental model that man could conceive, to the imagined persona of the deity. The theological depiction of the association between god and mankind, proposed by the priesthood, parallels the classical relationship between parents and their children. Man has painted a childish character picture of god that suits his wishes and desires, but is not confirmed by reality.

Nature testifies that god is dispassionate, but not loving or doting. It (god, as viewed through nature) is just, consistent, uncompromising, and very demanding but not cruel. And above all, in my opinion, god, as seen through nature, is constant, certain, dependable, and predictable; and this translates into the stability of the *natural order*, wherewith human intelligence can interact productively. If the natural order was devoid of certitude, human intelligence would be useless, lost, confused, in a void, and unable to calculate within a chaotic, amorphous *state of being* ungoverned by the natural paradigms of *cause and effect*.

The Biggest Lie Ever Told, 4th Edition

Chapter Two: Monotheism

There are those who believe that we are now entering a new age, an era meant for a New World Order.

Some of those who share this view preach that there are Signs in the Heavens to indicate that the time has arrived for profound *spiritual* and *political* changes on our planet. I have been familiar with this attitude for many years, in that my father was an avid astrologer. The *End of the World* means the end of an era, an *Age* or dominant credo. The credo that is now in its death throes and fighting with every force at its' disposal to expand and defend its creed is defined as monotheism. The **monotheists are** the so-called children of Abraham i.e. **Jews, Christians and Muslims**. The monotheists are the *unwitting* masters of political and religious tyranny; they demand that we worship and *serve only one god* and likewise they insist that ultimately, humanity will be ruled by one *theocratic* political government, after Judgment Day. **This tyranny is expressed in the monotheistic dogma that god will kill all disbelievers on judgment day or torment them incessantly in hell after death.**

The religious *doctrine* of the monotheist (i.e. the *doctrine* that they are the only correct worshippers of the only *true* god) tends to infuse itself into the political and social fabric of their societies. It follows in their thinking (whether openly acknowledged or not) that since their doctrine is allegedly the only true faith, that likewise their political and social systems must also be superior to all others. Consequently, they are implicitly justified by their deity in imposing their doctrines (political, financial and religious) upon the supposedly lost (non-believers) of the world. The Muslims and Christians tend to impose their doctrines by direct attack and the Jews act by methods of subversion. So this religious attitude of the monotheists indeed makes them the greatest menace to world peace, and I think that history verifies this. Of course the laity within the monotheistic systems are for the most part sincere and loving believers, who firmly believe that they are doing god's will by spreading his doctrine. My focus here is on the *underlying effect of the monotheistic doctrine*, and the attitude it engenders in those that adhere to this tyrannical dogma; which sounds so benevolent at the first hearing, but when thoughtfully analyzed is found to bear the seeds of religious and political tyranny. The indications are that our Founding Fathers realized this and therefore sought to limit the powers of the monotheists within our government, but the menace is ever-present.

History indicates that the philosophy of the monotheist came into distinct prominence under the sign of Aries about 4000 years ago amongst the Egyptians (witness sect of Akhenaton), and later the Hebrews. The philosophical power of the monotheists was further augmented under the astrological sign of Pisces, manifested by the sect of the Christians about 2000 years ago, and about 600 years later under Islam. The nature of the monotheists is to wipe out all opposition to their domination by demanding that the populations submit entirely to one omnipotent god (under one religious system) and concurrently to one world theocratic government (under one type of political system). The ultimate aim of the monotheists is to obliterate all political and financial independence worldwide by making them interdependent, with dominance exercised by the monotheists. Of course, political unity is greatly facilitated by cultural unity; hence the monotheists tend to use their religious dogma as a tool pursuant to cultural fusion.

The monotheists tend to demean and belittle the religious beliefs of others outside their own ranks. They label disbelievers as heathens and pagans who are doomed to total annihilation on the great Day of Judgment; hence history shows that the monotheists are capable of unspeakable cruelty toward various populations, and all in the name of one omnipotent god.

Astrological Ages

We are now entering the *Age of Aquarius* and there are some that believe that this is the era in which humanity shall be rescued from the onslaught of the monotheists. Aquarius is anticipated as an era of *enlightenment*, understanding and tolerance. The era of Aquarius is said to usher in the *Age of Reason* wherein **philosophical differences are respected and tolerated,** if not accepted. People shall worship or *not* worship god as they see fit and those who view themselves as the vicars of god will hopefully be converted to an attitude of tolerance and respect toward those outside the faith, so that we (freethinkers) can live in a semblance of peace and relative safety – devoid of the menacing threats of hellfire and damnation made by the monotheists.

According to the proponents of this philosophy (i.e. the belief that political, philosophical hegemony is linked to Astrological Ages), the history, proclivities, and hegemony of human civilization on earth is determined or gauged by changes in philosophical attitude that coincide approximately with the earth's precessional cycle. It takes about 25,920 years for this cycle to complete itself, and return to the point of its initiation.

A circle (cycle) is complete at 360 degrees. The equinox, during this period of 25,920 years, passes through the (12) twelve signs of the zodiac, starting at the cusp of Libra and Virgo and ending at the point of its commencement[2]

---

[2]PRECESSION MOVES WESTWARD THROUGH THE ZODIAC, THAT IS FROM THE THIRTIETH DEGREE OF A SIGN BACKWARD. THE BEGINNING OF THE 25,920 YEAR CYCLE RECOMMENCED 15,079 YEARS AGO (As of 1993 and assuming the 30th degree of Virgo as the commencement of the Great Year cycle). THE NEXT CYCLE OF AQUARIUS WILL BEGIN IN THE YEAR 2034 AD. A CHART OF THE CYCLES IS AS FOLLOWS:
PRECESSIONAL AGES:
VIRGO   COMMENCED 13086 BC
LEO   COMMENCED 10926 BC
CANCER COMMENCED 8766 BC
GEMINI COMMENCED 6606 BC
TAURUS COMMENCED 4446 BC
ARIES COMMENCED 2286 BC
PISCES COMMENCED 126 BC
ACQUARIUS WILL C0MMENCE 2034 AD
CAPRICORN WILL COMMENCE 4194 AD
SAGITTARIUS WILL COMMENCE 6354 AD
SCORPIO WILL COMMENCE 8514 AD
LIBRA WILL COMMENCE 10674 AD
AND VIRGO WILL REPEAT THE YEAR ONE 12834 AD

The Biggest Lie Ever Told, 4th Edition

By dividing the total cycle of 25,920 years by the number 12 (the 12 signs of the zodiac), we arrive at the figure of 2,160 years. The proponents teach that this period of time, (2,160 years) represents an Astrological Age.
Each *Age* represents more or less 30 degrees of the cycle and 2,160 years of time. During this span of time (2,160 years), the zodiacal sign identified by its position at the point of the vernal equinox is deemed the Ruling Sign under which the earth's inhabitants are governed for the period so indicated.
Accordingly, the philosophy (attitude) and the people (race, nation creed or region) who are the chief advocates of the attitude favored by the zodiacal sign of the age, shall be favored for dominance in world affairs.

We are now living in the Astrological Age of Pisces which commenced about 2,100 years ago. The early Christians saw themselves as the advocates of this Astrological Age that commenced 2100 years ago. History shows that the symbol of the *early* Christians was not only the Cross or Crucifix. The Symbol that represented their creed was the Fish[3]. They used this symbol (Fish) to proclaim themselves as masters of the *New Age*, represented by the zodiacal sign of Pisces
Once they were able to persuade the emperor Constantine to join forces with them; their road to world dominance was mapped. *It is impossible for a religious philosophy to achieve world dominance without a political-financial connection.* With Constantine in their camp, the Religious, Political, Financial Alliance was therefore formed --and the rest is history.

Now, in the 21st century, we have arrived at the dawn of the Age of Aquarius. We are at the cusp, the inflection point whereas the philosophical, financial and political forces of a dying astrological era are contending frantically against the emerging philosophy of the New Age. Pisces is setting and Aquarius is rising.

---

[3] The headdress (Miter) worn by the Catholic bishops symbolizes the Fish.

The Biggest Lie Ever Told, 4*th* Edition

The Dichotomy of Truth

Our quest is for truth; truth is evidentially provable. The very nature of a lie causes it (a lie) to lack provability, whereas the truth is physically and/or intellectually verifiable. It adds up correctly. It makes sense. It is reasonable, logically understandable, rationally acceptable, and able to withstand analysis and critical examination made by its proponents as well as its detractors.

The truth stands by reason of its own truthfulness. It needs no auxiliary supports. But beware of the lie (religious or otherwise), posing as the truth; because the advocates of the lie always request that we accept their jargon, not on the basis of its provability, but rather they encourage us to have faith. And not just good hearted down to earth faith, but rather a faith that is unreasonable, illogical, *a faith that requires us to actually twist the very fabric of normal thought processes in an adverse, abnormal way, to convince ourselves that somehow the lie is really the truth.* And *why should we*, as rational, intelligent, literate human beings, strain our mental faculties beyond the points of rationality, common sense, natural law and logic; distorting the contours of our brains in a vain attempt to make *sense* out of *nonsense*? This book is geared toward establishing the answer to that question.

There are some of us, *of more discerning intellect*, who believe that it is within reason for us to expect rational answers to certain probing questions concerning religion that may enter our minds from time to time.

We believe that to doubt and question the popular versions of god and religion is not synonymous to expressing doubt or criticism of god almighty.

We believe that it is possible to keep faith with god[4] and at the same time totally reject any concept of god that does not conform to logic and reason.

We believe that we should not be subject to accusations of heresy, hypocrisy, malicious intent, lack of faith, or atheism, simply because we

---

[4] I define god as the genesis of life, the god (natural) force that governs all – not as a personal deity.

seek understanding. All truth, I'm sure you agree, should be understandable and provable, and if not, why not?

The Unholy Trinity: Religion, Politics, and Economics

In this book, we shall explore how the *religious hierarchy altered the focus of the original religious scriptures for their own predatory purposes.* We shall explore how that Unholy Trinity (political, financial, religious alliance) has used the good name of religion to mislead, subjugate and destabilize the populations of the world.

Monotheism, at its core, is actually a political doctrine; it is, primitively, a nationalistic dogma devised, in one respect among others, to promote cultural unification pursuant ultimately to national unification, that is to say, cultural synthesis of various tribes, ethnicities, or cultures under one dominant culture i.e. god, which ultimately leads to political union under one flag, one cause, one nation or empire. Political leaders, historically (and to this day), have always used the banner of god when calling their people to unity for some notable task, be it aggression, national defense, or to combat some conditions that spawn an internal crisis, be they economic, social, or otherwise. They (the politicians, ancient and modern) always rally the populace by claiming that god is with us or god be with us to do this or that, that is to say whatever the championing cause may be. They evoke their god through lavish rhetoric or maudlin lamentations, avowing to the public that their one and only true god is with them to protect and lead them to victory. Monotheism and nationalism cannot be divorced; they are woven together just as one cloth. The nationalistic bent of monotheism is clearly and profusely expressed within the Torah, Bible and Quran – the politicians of these religions i.e. Judaism, Christianity, and Islam, as a matter of course, tend to inevitably link god with their political agendas, so as to inspire the support of their various populations.

Witness this quote concerning monotheism, from the late James Frazer, in his book Adonis, Attis Osirus, chapter 7, Osirus And The sun - which echoes my sentiments or we may say that my expressions are an echo of his prior inputs: *"For the religion of ancient Egypt may be described as a confederacy of local cults which, while maintaining against each other a certain measure of jealous and even hostile independence, were yet constantly subjected to the fusing and amalgamating influence of political centralization and philosophic thought. The history of religion appears to have largely consisted of a struggle between these opposite forces or tendencies. On the one side there was the conservative tendency to preserve the local cults with all their distinctive features, fresh, sharp, and crisp as they had been handed down from an immemorial past. On the other side there was the progressive tendency, favoured by the gradual fusion of the people under a powerful central government, first to dull the edge of these provincial distinctions, and finally to break them down completely and merge them in a single national religion"*. Monotheism is inherently intertwined with nationalism from its conception to this day. Monotheism is the child of centralized political systems, a means toward cultural fusion and national unity, with a single god as the tutelary deity and unifying spirit of the nation.

As I have noted repeatedly, monotheism is mythically derived from the symbolism of the sun as the all-powerful god, greater than all other heavenly gods (lights). This is the physical base on which this religious concept of monotheism is founded. The primary origin of this monotheistic concept is traceable to ancient Egypt. The ancient Egyptians elevated the god *Amen-Ra* (sun-god) to supremacy over all other deities. The Hebrews copied the concept by elevating their tribal deity *Yahweh* to the status of the only true god. Witness this quote from the late Egyptologist E. A. Wallis Budge in his book, The gods Of The Egyptians Volume Two: *"Thus by these means the priests of Amen succeeded in making their god, both theologically and politically, the greatest of the gods in the country...And when his royal devotees...carried war and conquest into Palestine and founded Egyptian cities there, the power and glory of Amen their god, who had enabled them to carry out this difficult work of successful invasion, became extraordinarily great...but the priests of Amen were not content with claiming that their god was one of the greatest of the deities of Egypt, for they proceeded to declare that there was no other god like him, and that he was the greatest of them all."* It's clear that monotheism and nationalism are joined at the hip, especially when the nationalistic culture is expansive and imperialistic. As the monotheists expand their territories, they always claim their successes are bequeathed by their deities. Such has been the case with the biblical Jews, the Christians and the Muslims – all claim that their aggressions (proselytizing) carry the blessings and sanctions of their omnipotent god (gods).

The eternal quest of humanity is the search for our father (creator) who seemingly abandoned us at birth. We are orphaned and our father is unknown – our mother is considered as the earth, because it is evident that we were created from the essence of this physical planet – but he/it (i.e. the Intelligence) that molded us and breathed the breath of life into us is unknown, and may always remain unknown. But our eternal quest is to search, to the ends of the universe, if necessary, for the father (creative intelligence) that abandoned or otherwise obscured itself from our physical eyes. But the claim of the monotheist is that our father (creator) is not unknown – they claim that the creator left a message for us in the form of revealed religion i.e. religion as a product of divine revelation to so-called prophets, and further that we shall be joined with our spiritual father in a spiritual world, to be entered into upon our departure from this physical existence. However we must submit to the rituals and customs dictated by monotheistic dogma in order to qualify for admittance into this spiritual afterlife. The net result of this form of belief is that our physical lives are controlled and managed by the proponents of this doctrine, and our spiritual lives are in question – based totally on faith, with no factual (provable) basis or support.

Biblical support of Monotheistic Tyranny

The terror of monotheism is that it is political as well as religious – it is a joint cultural force with an edict and command from their god to go forth to conquer and subdue. The Jewish god of the bible is clearly a tribal deity, a war god that advocates for his chosen, without compassion or just regards for the other members of the human family. The philosophy of world domination lies at the core of monotheism, a message to its adherents that they are the chosen of god and are destined to rule and control this planet. Let us review some biblical passages that reinforces this point:

Exodus 19:5 through Exodus 19:6

⁵Now therefore, if ye will obey my voice indeed, and keep my covenant, then ye shall be a peculiar treasure unto me above all people: for all the earth is mine: ⁶And ye shall be unto me a kingdom of priests, and an holy nation. These are the words which thou shalt speak unto the children of Israel.

Exodus 23:30 through Exodus 23:33

³⁰By little and little I will drive them out from before thee, until thou be increased, and inherit the land. ³¹And I will set thy bounds from the Red sea even unto the sea of the Philistines, and from the desert unto the river: for I will deliver the inhabitants of the land into your hand; and thou shalt drive them out before thee. ³²Thou shalt make no covenant with them, nor with their gods. ³³They shall not dwell in thy land, lest they make thee sin against me: for if thou serve their gods, it will surely be a snare unto thee.

There can be no doubt, the god depicted by the biblical verse above, is a tribal god, *that becomes a universal god by means of political/military conquest.* The crux, the central point of the covenant, as expressed above is that god promises territory and political sovereignty to the Hebrews if they will worship and obey him. The tribal gods prove their worth or superiority by bringing earthly success and domination to their subjects is the clear indication. The monotheistic god admits the existence of other gods, according to these and other biblical verses, but declares that he Yahweh is the true and greater god. This is clearly a reflection of ancient tribal culture when primitive tribes sought protection and guidance from their tutelary deities and touted them in times of war or conflict. And hence the political/military successes of a tribe tended to vindicate the worthiness and power of their god and likewise expanded the theological presence of their deity concurrent with the political territorial expansion of the adherents to the tribal deity.

Aggression is inherent to monotheism - political, social, military and financial hostility and interference into the affairs of non-believers is central to this belief system - and the bible is adamant on this point. According to the bible *non-believers should be killed and oppressed without mercy* in this life by the true believers and are doomed to total annihilation or perhaps eternal suffering in the next life. Take note of these verses from the bible that verify my contention:

Deuteronomy 13:1 through Deuteronomy 13:3

¹If there arise among you a prophet, or a dreamer of dreams, and giveth thee a sign or a wonder, ²And the sign or the wonder come to pass, whereof he spake unto thee, saying, Let us go after other gods, which thou hast not known, and let us serve them; ³Thou shalt not hearken unto the words of that prophet, or that dreamer of dreams...

Deuteronomy 13:5 through Deuteronomy 13:9

⁵And that prophet, or that dreamer of dreams, shall be put to death; because he hath spoken to turn you away from the LORD your god...

⁶If thy brother, the son of thy mother, or thy son, or thy daughter, or the wife of thy bosom, or thy friend, which is as thine own soul, entice thee secretly, saying, Let us go and serve other gods, which thou hast not known, thou, nor thy fathers; ⁷Namely, of the gods of the people which are round about you, nigh unto thee, or far off from thee, from the one end of the earth even unto the other end of the earth; ⁸Thou shalt not consent unto him, nor hearken unto him; neither shall thine eye pity him, neither shalt thou spare, neither shalt thou conceal him: ⁹But thou shalt surely kill him; thine hand shall be first upon him to put him to death, and afterwards the hand of all the people.

Deuteronomy 13:12 through Deuteronomy 13:15

¹²If thou shalt hear say in one of thy cities, which the LORD thy god hath given thee to dwell there, saying, ¹³... Let us go and serve other gods, which ye have not known; ¹⁴Then shalt thou inquire, and make search, and ask diligently; and, behold, if it be truth, and the thing certain, that such abomination is wrought among you; ¹⁵Thou shalt surely smite the inhabitants of that city with the edge of the sword, destroying it utterly, and all that is therein, and the cattle thereof, with the edge of the sword.

The Biggest Lie Ever Told, 4ᵗʰ Edition

According to our preachers and ministers, the bible is a direct revelation from god – and in his book (Bible, Torah, Quran) we are ordered by god almighty to murder those that do not share our belief. And not only are we ordered by this monotheistic god-demon to kill non-believers, which is horror enough actually - but also, as indicated by verses 12 through 15, we are told to search out those that disbelieve, to make *inquisitions* into the affairs of the citizenry and to execute those that are proven wayward.

This, I contend, is the Terror Of Monotheism – intolerance, aggression and merciless hostility toward those that choose not to accept this primitive doctrine. **You must read further** on what god, according to the bible directs his servants to render unto non-believers:

Deuteronomy 7:2
²And when the LORD thy god shall deliver them before thee; thou shalt smite them, and utterly destroy them; thou shalt make no covenant with them, nor show mercy unto them:

Deuteronomy 7:5 through Deuteronomy 7:6
⁵But thus shall ye deal with them; ye shall destroy their altars, and break down their images, and cut down their groves, and burn their graven images with fire. ⁶For thou art an holy people unto the LORD thy god: the LORD thy god hath chosen thee to be a special people unto himself, above all people that are upon the face of the earth.

Deuteronomy 7:16
¹⁶And thou shalt consume all the people which the LORD thy god shall deliver thee; thine eye shall have no pity upon them: neither shalt thou serve their gods; for that will be a snare unto thee.

Deuteronomy 7:22 through Deuteronomy 7:25
²²And the LORD thy god will put out those nations before thee by little and little: thou mayest not consume them at once, lest the beasts of the field increase upon thee. ²³But the LORD thy god shall deliver them unto thee, and shall destroy them with a mighty destruction, until they be destroyed. ²⁴And he shall deliver their kings into thine hand, and thou shalt destroy their name from under heaven: there shall no man be able to stand before thee, until thou have destroyed them. ²⁵The graven images of their gods

shall ye burn with fire: thou shalt not desire the silver or gold that is on them, nor take it unto thee, lest thou be snared therein: for it is an abomination to the LORD thy god.

These verses are definite and unambiguous – the biblical god clearly directs his adherents to exact a scorched earth campaign against those that reject the doctrine of monotheism and would rather worship or not worship in accordance with their own individual consciousness. This war-god of monotheism even promises and urges his flock to consume and decimate the worlds disbelievers with planned precision, that is in degrees, step by malicious step, little by treacherous little is the biblical instruction. This, I contend is the terror of monotheism, the scourge of monotheism, that it is, at its religious core, a political (theocratic) system of forced indoctrination. It (monotheism) is fundamentally a form of imperialism or at the least an adjunct to imperialism, defined as a system of territorial expansion, nation building or the expansion of national influence – whether through direct control or through coercion. Sovereignty (legal government) gives the monotheists control of the body - and monotheistic doctrine itself gives them control of the mind and serves as a unifying national spirit. This is the hard truth that we must contend with, and place in proper perspective. And this, historically, has been a function of monotheistic doctrine, that is the enhancing of national and regional cohesion through cultural assimilation.

True biblical monotheism does not allow for peaceful coexistence with people or societies of different philosophical or religious persuasions. God's command to the monotheists, according to the bible, is to overcome them by stratagem or by direct aggression. This is the message of the biblical verses that I have submitted for your perusal, and this message rings with resounding clarity throughout the so-called Holy Scriptures of the Jews, Christians and Muslims. The Jews are certainly in compliance with this biblical godly directive. They (Hebrews) most certainly have a stratagem by which they have and are consuming the world of the gentiles, little by little as their god directs. The Christians and Muslims are also in compliance, as both have as cardinal tenets within their doctrines the advocacy of proselytization.

The Biggest Lie Ever Told, 4th Edition

Monotheism is a scourge, and the scourge of monotheism is the arrogant and repressive doctrine of Jews, Christians and Muslims which postulates that the god of their faith (faiths) is the only true god and that spiritual salvation can only be obtained from within their ranks or through them, as the bona fide agents of the only true god. This elitist tyrannical conception was spawned by Jewish style monotheism, and is absolutely deplorable, in my opinion. This attitude, of the monotheists, is a manifestation of religious bigotry to the highest degree. And this religious bigotry has engendered and continues to sow the seeds of political, social, financial and racial bigotry within every fabric of monotheistic society and tends to contaminate other social structures that ordinarily would not share these biases. .

Any society founded on monotheism is by its very nature a meddlesome community, intent on interfering in the affairs of others and seeking to subvert or override the social/political systems of others, pursuant to the ostensibly high-minded goals of help and improvement. This is the clarion call of monotheism, that is to bring all others into the one so-called true path (faith) – and that translates into subversion, aggression, and interference into the social structures of nonbelievers, with a godly edict to do so.

Mark 16:15 through Mark 16:16

¹⁵And he said unto them, Go ye into all the world, and preach the gospel to every creature. ¹⁶He that believeth and is baptized shall be saved; but he that believeth not shall be damned.

Matthew 28:19

¹⁹Go ye therefore, and teach all nations, baptizing them in the name of the Father, and of the Son, and of the Holy Ghost:

Matthew 24:14

¹⁴And this gospel of the kingdom shall be preached in all the world for a witness unto all nations; and then shall the end come.

Monotheists seemingly have thoughtful and admiral concepts concerning the equitable application of law, respect for individual freedom and liberty and property rights etc. Their moral precepts are laudable for the most part, in my opinion, but rarely lived up to. Their sense of justice is widely proclaimed (as if those within their ranks are the only true proponents of justice) but not universally applied, actually it is favored for those of faith. This is reflective, perhaps subliminally, of their religious doctrine that states clearly god's final condemnation of all disbelievers on that great Judgment Day. This attitude, that people of different religious persuasions are actually in rebellion against the true faith or are somehow victims of the wiles of Satan, and thereby servants of the devil, opens the door to any manner of injustices and oppression toward *non*-monotheist.

If and when the monotheists adhere faithfully to their religious concepts, which encourage them to spread their doctrine to the far reaches of the world, they in affect become a menace to all cultures that would like to be left alone to worship or not worship according to their own customs. This proselytizing of culture and faith is a certain formula for world unrest and contention, so long as it is pursued. The ancients knew this and consequently, practiced a system of henotheism, that gave tolerance and respect to diverse philosophical and religious views - but monotheism (a useful tool of imperialist) broke the cycle, and now it (monotheism) must be broken before peace and stability can be restored, in my opinion. All religious philosophy is reflective of a material base, a foundation anchored in matter (the physics of nature). *Spirits based on Physics* is my trademark phrase in reference to this premise of dualism, i.e. all spiritual concepts have a counterpart in physical nature. The physical counterpart of monotheism is the all-conquering light of the sun. The sun does not allow any other heavenly light to exist within its domain. The sun not only destroys darkness with the dawn of its day, but it also blots out all of the night lights (lesser gods) - the starry and planetary lights of darkness are destroyed, without mercy, by the sun at its dawning.

All of our religious concepts are engendered by physical nature or are reflective of physical nature– it can be no other way, because we are physical creatures ourselves and are molded by our environment. We are forced to live within the limitations set by our natural environment and if we explore beyond these confines, we must carry a portion of our earthly universe with us, in order to sustain ourselves. Our base is physical and our spiritual concepts are built upon this material base, hence the nature of dualism is revealed in this aspect of spirit and matter. Of course this is debatable as there are many that insist the Spirit is the first creation or bases of creation that preceded Matter, and that god is spirit. I don't know which came first, and will never *Know*. It is my belief however, that spirit and matter are interdependent and have always coexisted and will forever be joined or associated. I do know, that you and I are *physical beings* and are only capable of conceiving spiritual things because *we in the first instance physically exist* as physical beings, and can think (spiritualize) – this is reality. We can investigate matter, analyze matter and scrutinize matter – everything that is physical is subject to our intelligent evaluation, but *that which is spiritual can only be conjectured upon* and will forever prove theoretical, regardless of how much faith one may have in his or her conclusions. A basis does not exist in the physical universe for proving or dispassionately evaluating religious concepts that are alleged to have sprung from a spiritual base, because the spiritual is not subject to natural laws of proof but rather is considered supernatural. The dualistic approach, as I see it, stipulates that all spiritual concepts, in order to be valid, must have a physical counterpart. This dualistic concept proposes that this physical universe is a material copy of the presumed spiritual universe or vice versa. The spiritual is not subject to natural laws of proof but rather is considered supernatural (i.e. beyond physical/natural laws of proof), so without a physical reference by which to analyze the spiritual we tend to wonder into wild imaginary, ungrounded speculations, and this leads to irrationality. However the ancients, in their wisdom, when discerning and molding that which was spiritual, used the physics of nature, in accordance with their developing understanding of it, as their guide and model, is my contention – and hence all religious philosophy descended to us from the ancients is reflective of a *perceived* physical basis, according to the gnosis.

Chapter Three: Origin Of Religion

Now, on the subject of Religion, Mythology and Environment.
There are people, of rational intellect, who believe that religion springs
forth from ancient pagan myth. Although there is evidence to support this
claim, this assertion requires explanation. Of course, many of us understand
that religion indeed possesses mythological aspects. Nevertheless this
mythology was not produced by myth,[5] but rather as an **allegorical
representation of the environment.** In the same way that most legends
have a basis of truth, so it is with Religious Myth.
My prime purpose, within this book, is to produce logical evidence
of the true evolution of religion - **from astronomical and environmental
symbolism.**

I must emphasize and will continually re-emphasize the importance of
understanding the truth of the process of religious evolution, i.e. *from the
environment (veiled by symbolism), to Myth, to Ritualism, to
Traditionalism, to Modern Religious Dogma.*
When we analyze our modern myths, *from the perspective of our ancestors*
who formulated these ideas, we find cohesion, deductive logic, and an
accurate reflection of esoteric symbolism.
But in order to understand the origins of myth, based on allegorical
illustrations of the environment, we must (mentally) go back in time. We
must, (for the sake of understanding), put ourselves in the shoes of the
originators of primitive or evolving religious culture, and view the world as
they must have seen it, so many thousands of years ago. We must

---

[5]The traditional lay concept of the word Myth is a *fanciful tale or story*, not necessarily related to actual truth or history.
It is important for the reader to understand that originally, religious myth was the symbolical and allegorical rendering of
information concerning the activity of the natural environment (primarily celestial). This allegory was based on empirical
studies of the universe, and therefore born or produced by people with an intimate knowledge of Reality (natural
phenomena).

temporarily adopt their attitudes and imagine ourselves existing in their era, without the knowledge, universal perspective, and environmental understanding that we, in this day, possess.

We must understand that, to the mind of primitive humankind, the primary world was not this vast globe (earth) that nourishes us (its children) approximately 25,000 miles in circumference; no! Their world was the limited vicinity in which they lived and worked, or were familiar with by travel or trade. Their world was their region, only a speck of the real world, as we know it today. And it follows in logical progression, that their gods were not world gods, in the sense that we view the world today. Their gods were the gods of their regional world. And their concept of god, quite understandably, reflected their fears, needs, and hopes, and dependency on the natural environment.

Primitive religion or myth can easily be put into the categories of sun god worship and nature god worship. They worshipped the sun because of their need of the sun and its light, its warmth. The sun was the lord and ruler of the physical world, the life giver and the destroyer of the demons of night. So when primitive man imaged god, he was imaged with spiritual attributes that paralleled those of the physical sun. god in the spirit was the light of the world, the destroyer of demons of darkness, the savior, the healer and the raiser of the dead, etc.

Primordial man viewed the sun (fire) as the king of the heavens, the life giver, destroyer and preserver. The sun is the ruler (Lord) of our solar system and the source and sustainer of all life within its domain. The ancients imagined the *sun as the physical counterpart of god in the spirit*. All that the sun is to the world of matter is in direct parallel to god as a spiritual concept was their contention. The physical sun (fire) gives life to the dead earth and sight to the blind (by destroying darkness). It (fire, sun) purifies our atmosphere and regenerates the life forces of nature. They envisioned god in the *Spirit* as a direct reflection of the god (sun) of *Matter*. This goes to the core meaning of worshipping the sun (fire) as a symbol of the spiritual god.

They worshipped the gods of Nature - rain, earth, crops, or the forces that they believed stimulated these elements, because these environmental forces were the gods (controllers) of their destiny.

They worshipped some *nature gods* out of fear. They did not understand or comprehend the forces of nature as we do today. Early man lacked the knowledge necessary to intellectually analyze the causative factors behind nature's rampages, therefore they imagined that drought, earthquakes, hurricanes, tornadoes, floods, volcanic eruptions, pestilence, epidemics and the like were caused by gods gone mad or by demonic spirits.

They believed that all actions, whether human, animal or environmental, were motivated by spirits and that some spirits were benevolent while others were demonic. And, of course, this concept led to the belief that all sickness, sin and environmental trauma were caused by evil spirits i.e. people, animals or elements of nature that were *possessed* with evil spirits (demons). To counteract these evil spirits, the ancients developed rituals, prayers, chants and various ceremonies that were used to scare away or caste out the evil spirits (demons). This is superstition veiled under the guise of religion.

Also, all primitive religious systems, contained, in part, elements of ritual sacrifice.

The ritual sacrifice was a cure-all, an all around panacea used by the early devotees to influence the good gods as well as the bad gods. They perceived that by making sacrifice to the good gods, they would keep them happy--a gift to the gods, in order to stay on their good side, as it where. As for the bad gods, the ritual sacrifice served as a bribe to forestall his (the gods) anger or wrath.[6]

In the minds of primitive mankind; when the gods became angry with humanity, they (the gods) punished them by interfering with their attainment of life's vital necessities, i.e. food, clothing and shelter; by #1 -

---

[6]Sir James George Frazer, in his book *The Golden Bough,* describes the victims of these sacrifices as scapegoats. His book is replete with examples of how the ritual sacrifice was used by primitives to expiate the sins of their communities

turning the forces of nature against mankind (i.e. earthquakes, floods, storms etc.) #2 - depriving mankind of essential elements and food (i.e. through drought, blight, etc.) or #3-direct attack, in the form of disease, or some invading foreign army causing widespread death And/or destruction.

They noticed, in accordance with their primitive logic, that the final outcome of that which they perceived to be god's anger toward them (the bottom line, if you will) was punishment.

Therefore they imagined, and likewise were led to believe by the priesthood, that if they *showed repentance through sacrifice* that such action might forestall the wrath and punishment of their imagined deities. This is superstition born out of ignorance.

Evolution of Religion

In order to properly evaluate and trace the evolution of religion and its impact on our modern religious philosophy, we must go far back in time to the *earliest anthropological and archeological indications of the ascendancy of man* from roving bands of scattered families, foraging and hunting for foodstuffs wherever possible, to nascent establishments of settled tribal communities.

The history of ancient mans emergence from the *nomadic state* into *settled communities* with organizational structure, agriculture, animal husbandry, and the partitioning of permanent hereditary duties to families and/or members of the community, the nascent formations of Military, Royal, Ecclesiastical and Artisan Class structures with centralized authority and rules of conduct is key to pinpointing the embryonic cultural and social traditions that over the millennia would eventually evolve into the social force popularly known today as revealed religion, inclusive of its social creeds and spiritual concepts. In fact all forms of religion practiced in this (our) era can be traced to this same type source or origin. *Our religious philosophies are an evolutionary reflection of man's historical interaction with nature, shielded in myth and fable.* These myths and fables of the distant past have evolved into our modern religious concepts. There is no truth to the concept of *Revealed Religion* (Revelation From a god (supernatural spirit) to a messenger (prophet)) – all religious beliefs are the result of mankind's societal evolution, and the key to interpreting the myths and symbols embodied therein is found when we accurately separate actual history from mythical history, and then evaluate the actual history and its mythological counterparts dispassionately – and this task is not easily accomplished.

I *must* re-emphasize that the key to unlocking the veiled theological mysteries of the distant past and thereby shedding great and illuminating light upon the religious enigmas of the present, lay in *uncovering* and *analyzing* the early social structures of the *first settled agricultural communities* emerging from pre-history. That is *not* to say that mankind did not possess god concepts in his nomadic phases – most certainly he did, if we accept that the *belief* in the unknown creator (spirit) is innate in humans. Natural history and Time have no beginning, no origin that we can point to, no year one (or 0) so to speak, and herein lays the eternal unfulfilled quest of the *enlightened* of mankind – to find this Father of our beginnings with the hope that such knowledge will unveil our purpose and destiny.

The evolution of religious thought from primitive times to the present is explainable but entails a dispassionate study of history and some common unbiased logic. The first step in this long process of religious evolution started with the emergence of the priesthood. They evolved from a class of *Star Gazers* and *Naturalist* whose appointed hereditary duty, within ancient society, was the recording and forecasting of seasonal transitions. They (the Stargazers) signaled the planting of seeds and the harvesting of the crops. They studied and measured the cycles of time and the seasons by observing and recording the comings and goings of the celestial entities – and noting the terrestrial associations (rainfall, flooding, drought, animal migration, etc.) that accompanied the arrival and departure of these cosmic entities (stars, planets, asterisms, etc.) to and from specified coordinates. They were the first astronomers and meteorologists and masters of mathematics, which was a required skill within their ranks.

These early societies were stratified – whatever caste or class that an individual was born of determined his destiny throughout life, that is to say the obligation of the child to his society and rank or position within the society was inherited from the parents. This worked fine for the stargazers, in that their pivotal profession as keepers of the time blossomed intellectually far, far beyond the scope of the masses. Their abilities became prodigious over time, to the amazement of the common classes. They not only predicted the coming of the seasons in their order, but they forecasted the rains, the floods, solar and lunar eclipses, the phases of the moon and declinations of the sun and the Impact of their transits upon the land and its inhabitants. They charted the heavens, grouped the stars and named them. These stargazers garnered this phenomenal knowledge and ability at a time when the general public was overwhelmingly illiterate – they became a lordly class unto themselves. They cherished their supreme position and it was, of course, preserved within the caste system that prevailed. But the security afforded by Class distinction was not enough for these elitists who through superior knowledge had de facto control of the ancient emerging world which over time would evolve from community farms into city-states and into empires. So they decided to encode their knowledge into cryptic (symbolical) form – they invented the language of esoteric mythology, symbolism and allegory –a symbolic language that could only be correctly interpreted by those who had undergone mystical initiations within their Secret Societies or Fraternities.

This ancient mystical code that was incorporated to *preserve* and *enshroud* the wisdom and knowledge of the emerging sacerdotal class of antiquity is the archetypical mythology that has blinded common society spiritually down to this day. This mythology at the exoteric level is literal nonsense but within its esoteric folds resides the supreme wisdom of the ages.

When Primitive man began to settle in agricultural communities, it became necessary that they regulate their farming and animal husbandry within the constraints of the seasonal changes. It therefore was necessary for the tribes to assign some individuals (stargazers) to devote themselves to the study and tracking of the coming seasons and of course to financially support these appointees who worked for the common good. The offices or positions of these appointees (stargazers) were hereditary and their scientific knowledge increased exponentially and was kept strictly secret, not shared with the other levels of society. Their cosmic prognostications took on the aspect of secret wisdom; and of course it was to their advantage to conceal their methods and knowledge so as to secure their privileged position in society. So as society evolved religiously, over thousands of years, these astronomers and mathematicians (calculators of the seasons) became the primary ministers of religious thought, thus the sacerdotal class was begun.

In order to clearly understand the evolution of religion from the science of astronomy, we must recognize that this process of religious evolution covered many thousands of years. The actual birth of the process is forever lost in antiquity, and the motivations of those who engineered and in later times diverted (or modified) the *focus* of the process (in terms the mythical-religious illustration of a physical reality) were varied. Originally, the primitive stargazers (astronomers) of primordial times were certainly dedicated to the common good of their tribes. But as the centuries and millenniums passed and their intellectual advances so greatly exceeded those of the general population, they succumbed to the inevitable temptations of avarice and lust for power. They applied their superior knowledge in a way that enhanced and secured their privileged status. First of all their positions as Timekeepers were hereditary, so this served to keep their advanced knowledge of mathematics, astronomy and meteorology confined within restricted ranks. But this did not satisfy them – they also established secret codes and symbols so that their knowledge was elevated to another language that was incomprehensible to the uninitiated. They covered the possibilities of dissension within their families also so as to prevent the unworthy or untrustworthy access to this esoteric wisdom; they established secret and closed societies for those that were chosen as candidates to be trained in the mysteries of their esoteric wisdom. The candidates had to pass certain arduous test, which served to gauge their loyalty and dedication to the inner circle. They also had to swear life and death oaths - that they would never reveal the secrets of their closed societies. Even when the candidates were accepted, all the doors of the esoteric wisdom were not opened to them. The ancient Priests established a tier system for the gradual advancement of the potential hierophants – knowledge was unveiled to the candidates in degrees and each advancement required tasks of qualification.

The ancient priesthood of primordial times and early civilization possessed an environmental knowledge that rivals our understanding of the environment here in the 21ˢᵗ century. They possessed this knowledge (higher mathematics, astronomy, geography, meteorology) at a time (in pre-history) when the great majority of the population was illiterate. The ignorant masses were superstitious and uneducated with little or no understanding of the cycles of nature and the causes of the seasons. And this ignorance suited the tactics of the priesthood just fine. The esoteric wisdom was maintained and controlled by the priesthood and shared somewhat with the royalty. As religion evolved from astronomy i.e. the symbolic illustration of the science of astronomy, the priesthood used their advanced scientific knowledge to mesmerize and astonish the masses.

So as the priesthood (this sacerdotal society that over hundreds and thousands of years had evolved from a class of *timekeepers*, star gazers, weather forecasters) began to proselytize the public and formulate the religious tenets of the various societies, they touted themselves as the vicars of the gods, as god's emissaries to the populations of earth. The priesthood had the power (knowledge) and ability to actuate and perpetuate this chicanery- they would astound the people, for example, by declaring that at a certain time and location at their command, the moon shall blot out the light of the sun, or perhaps they would predict a lunar eclipse or the onslaught of turbulent weather or drought. All this they could predict by means of their scientific knowledge, but in the minds of the ignorant masses these priest, soothsayers and witchdoctors were visualized as true emissaries of the gods - how else could they possess such powers were the thoughts of the benighted.

I would add that the special dates that were established for harvesting or planting or whatever, may have at first only been secular notations on the calendar, but over time these special days became sacred days and eventually deities were attached to these sacred days as well as religious ceremonies which served to offer sacrifice or obeisance to the deities so designated. It also follows that the priesthood became very adept at the science of architecture and that religious buildings and monuments were therefore designed to help aid in the effort of tracking time. The orientation of the structures were laid so as to measure the movements of the sun, moon and stars and thereby give notice to the initiated of the entrances and exits of the seasons.

Originally, the tasks assigned to the ancient Time Keepers (Stargazers) of these fledgling agricultural communities was to track the seasons and notify the public of the appropriate time to sow their seeds and of the appropriate time to harvest the crops. This information was vital to the survival of these newly settled hamlets of antiquity, making their first attempts at transition from the hand to mouth existence of nomadism. And as these ancient Timekeepers recorded their observations by the customary methods of oral traditions or markings on natural landmarks etc. they had in fact entered the embryonic stages of the science of astronomy, and concurrently (and unknowingly) laid the foundation upon which the world's religions would be fashioned in the millennia that followed.

Of course the system of tracking the seasons by using stars as *signposts* to announce their (seasons) comings and goings worked fine, just as it does to this very day. But anciently, as the system of using stars to mark the skies and announce the entrances and exits of the seasons became customary and second nature to the peoples, the original purposes (or understanding of how and why the system was initiated) became lost or clouded in the minds of the masses. As the years rolled by, the custom of searching the heavens for particular asterisms to signal various agricultural and related activities became *ritualized*. After a while, in the public mind, it was not enough spiritually or psychologically to just run into the fields and sow or harvest when the appropriate heavenly signpost appeared on the horizon. They fashioned that a celebration was in order and festivities and the like.

As more years rolled by, just celebrating the arrival of the starry signposts became spiritually insufficient and psychologically non-fulfilling – *so much depended upon the arrival of the stars* that announced not only the agricultural activities, but marked the seasons for rain and sprouting fields and forest and spawning fish, animal migration and so forth. The masses began to look to the starry signposts not only as markers of the seasons but rather as *Bringers* of the seasons. They imagined that their *rituals of celebration* that greeted the annual arrivals of various stars or star groups (constellations) did not carry enough glory (significance) for these momentous occasions. Now praise and supplication were in order – the starry signposts at this point took on aspects of divine deities, in the minds of the superstitious masses, deities worthy of praise and laudable beyond limits. The stars were no longer viewed as only heavenly lights but also as temples of the gods – these stars were imagined to house the spirits of the divinities and were not only worthy of praise but praise was required. The stars were the first celestial entities to be ranked as deities, according to the scholars that have researched these matters, then came Lunar deities, followed by the Solar deities – they (the stars) were imagined as residents of heaven and the bringers of fair weather and bounty and rain and blessings to their human subjects.

The above written expresses the early stages of *human* development and also of human *religious* development – and all is innately connected with the cosmos, the heavenly vault of the skies. The link between all is the element of Time, that is the tracking and measurement of Time, and Time tracking is the basis on which all scripture is formulated. The scriptures are, in fact, registries of astronomical phenomena written in a mythological format, plain and simple.

It is logically evident that Star Worship evolved from the *ritualizing* of the system of using stars and asterisms (groups of stars) as markers so as to track time. The stars were used to signal the comings and goings of the seasons, and to locate the position of the sun on its annual journey. These stars, asterisms, common constellations and zodiacal constellations enabled early man to identify the cardinal points and use other assorted stars and constellations as signpost for measuring the span in between cardinal points and tracking the sun as it traveled throughout the year. This was of obvious importance so that early civilization could successfully plant and harvest crops as well as for other reasons such as migration, animal husbandry, food storage and export and so on and so on.

It is very easy to understand that by making these *signal* days[7] of the stars into holidays and festivals their remembrance was assured. And it follows that as society became more and more religious that these *signal* days (that were a matter of life and death in terms of their importance to agriculture) – that these *signal* days would over time evolve into religious or sacred days dedicated to certain deities (stars) that were now not just *indicators* of the seasons but actually viewed as the bringers and causers of the seasons. After humanity deified the stars, it of course followed in natural progression that the deities became deserving of worship and sacrifices. And in this we have the evolution of religious rituals based on primitive astronomical observations that were geared to tracking time in order to assure propitious agricultural and related enterprises.

The first stellar deities were depicted as animals, some malevolent and some benevolent. They chose animals names for the various constellations, animals whose presence or activity was somehow associated with the season of the stars heliacal appearance on the eastern horizon, such as the heliacal rising of the Dog-Star *Sirius*, barking its announcement of the dog days of summer. A stars heliacal descent on the western horizon was also a reference indicator and the stars that transited the midnight meridian served as another reference coordinate for tracking time. The characteristics of the animals would in some way be associated with the concurrent activity or season that the stars arrival on the horizon was found to indicate. For example, the bull deity was associated with fertility – hence a Spring constellation indicating new birth. The lion was in some instances associated with ferocious heat – hence it was a summer constellation. The Virgin with a stalk of Wheat may have been associated with harvesting and so forth. The deities were not limited to just one symbolic indication. As

---

[7] Of course the signal days were the days marked by the appearance of certain stars that signaled that the time had arrived for some agricultural or other related activity to take place

time passed the deities became humanized in form but maintained animal attributes as part of their guise, perhaps in the attire of the deity or some ornament. And in many cases human and animal anatomies were fused so as to create a symbolic portrayal that was part animal and part human in visual appearance. I'm thinking mainly of ancient Egyptian symbolism as I write this.

Of course some stars (deities) were indicators of propitious events (seasons) while other stars (deities) were witnessed with foreboding. The benevolent stars (deities) were greeted with great offerings of flowers, foodstuffs, dancing and various tangible demonstrations of gratitude and welcoming. But the ominous stars (deities) were served with blood sacrifices, fasting, self-mutilation and various rituals that were designed to appease and placate the wrathful deities. Our religious rituals of today have sprung from the sources that I have just described.

As we enter into the study of religious development, from pre-history to the present, it is vitally important that we understand the premise, by which the truth can be accurately deduced.

Modern religious fallacies are not based totally on the fanciful imaginations of savage primitives. Religious myths (i.e. the misguided acceptance of myths as historical truths) also result from distortions and misapplications, misunderstandings of the symbolism embodied in primitive rituals and customs.

Religious evolution amongst the Laity

The basic premise of our attack at clarifying and properly understanding the attitude of the **laity** anciently is: # 1-In the beginning there was a *Contentious Environment* (nascent societies surrounded by a hostile environment without a developed understanding of the causal forces of nature) which led to # 2-*Myth*, the fanciful creation (based on superstition) of gods and Demons as the Controllers of the Forces and Elements within their environment. To # 3- *Ritualism* - the establishment of rituals and sacrifices to appease or please their imagined deities and demons. To # 4-*Tradition* - which is the continued reverence of outmoded rituals and customs by a society where scientific knowledge has increased to the point that they should know better; nevertheless the Laity tends to continue the superstitious practices anyway, because of a religious indoctrination cultivated over the millennia and habitually perpetuated. To # 5, *Modern Organized Religion* - The political, financial, religious leadership alliance, that finds it to their advantage to perpetuate the ignorance of the masses for purposes of control, organization, defense, aggression, and the accumulation and protection of their (leadership) wealth.

So here we have the five progressive steps from prehistory to modern religious philosophy; that is, in the beginning there was the natural environment that was not scientifically understood, which stimulated myth as a *make do* explanation of natures mysterious forces. **The myth engendered ritualism** as a means of reference and supplication to the mythical deities. **Ritualism produced traditionalism**, wherein a society continues to observe worthless rituals, which have been invalidated over time by reason of societies intellectual advancement; but nevertheless (these rituals) are maintained out of habit and societies misguided allegiance to the primitive sentiments of past generations.

And finally, out of the aforementioned quagmires, there have arisen **classes of acquisitive overlords, allied politically, financially, and religiously,** that find it to their advantage to perpetuate the spiritual and religious ignorance of the general populations for their (leadership alliance) own selfish (parasitic) purposes.

When we examine the Christian religion; we find that the crux of that creed, the essential element of Christian dogma is that Jesus Christ was the Sacrificial Lamb, that Christ's life was sacrificed in order that we, the world, might live:

John 1:29 ----"behold, the Lamb of god, which taketh away the sin of the world." Matthew 20:28 -----"son of man come---to give his life as a ransom for many." Matthew 26:28-----"my blood---which is shed for many for the remission of sins".

I have sighted these bible verses in order to give emphasis to the point that I shall shortly make. Actually I don't think that any devout Christian would deny that one of the most important tenets of Christian doctrine is that Christ life was sacrificed for the sins of the world.

As I explained earlier, concerning the evolution of religion; the process entailed five stages, commencing with humanity steeped in *ignorance*, which was compounded by *superstition* (myths), which led to the *ritualized reverence* of mythical deities, which (rituals) overtime became *traditionalized*; and it is upon this base that our *modern religious concepts* have been founded. The laity of *Old* did not have an accurate understanding of the potentially oppressive forces of nature; therefore they imagined angry spirits and gods as the instigators of these elements.

The sacrificial lamb or ox or virgin, warrior, whatever, was a gift to god to bribe him, a ransom, given by the faithful so that they might be spared (saved) from future punishment.[8] This myth (that god needs a sacrifice to appease him) grew out of superstitious ritualism. When we ask ourselves the question, -- why on earth does the *creator* god of this universe need the sacrificial death of someone in order to delay or spare the world's destruction; our minds become confused. There is no intelligent rationale to this dogma. This religious belief only becomes understandable, when we realize that it is a carryover from the traditional sacrificial rites of the preceding cultures. As they proceeded from idolatry into so-called modern religious culture, they brought with them their traditions (traditionalism)

---

[8]Read "the golden bough" by James Frazer. His book contains a substantial amount of information on ancient ritual sacrifice.

and incorporated these traditions into their new beliefs. Hence, their sacrificial lambs, goats, oxen, and miscellaneous animal and human scapegoats of prior days were consummated into one sacrificial lamb, which they called the Christ.

Religious sacrifice is as old as humanity itself; animal and human sacrificial customs cross all ancient cultures. The so-called sacred sacrifice of Jesus Christ upon the cross is simply a modernized copy of the old human sacrifices of our heathen past, when human victims were bludgeoned upon altars before man-made or imagined pagan gods as a payment or ransom for tribal sins, so as to spare these communities from the potential wrath of their deities. Anciently, one of the most popular sacrificial animals was the lamb. Now they have transformed this sacrificial animal into the human form of Christ, and they call him (Christ) the *lamb of god*, which only means that the animal sacrifice has been humanized. Christ is idolized as a sacrificial *son of god* that is killed (sacrificed) so as to spare humanity from the wrath of a higher god, termed *god the father*. Christ is alleged to have died (been sacrificed) to save the world from their sins; this is in exact duplication of the customs of our pagan ancestors who slaughtered their sacrificial victims upon raised altars before effete counterfeit deities in order to save their tribal communities from the fantasized wraths of their seemingly praiseworthy but also feared pagan gods. Human sacrifice was the most appalling of all the ancient pagan rituals, by far, in my opinion; but nevertheless we, in this so-called modern age, applaud the alleged sacrificial death of one that we call the Christ – it is the same old pagan custom practiced under a new religious guise.

The Biggest Lie Ever Told, 4th Edition

Chapter Four: Biblical Myths

Now, for a concrete example of a tale that, in the beginning, was based on the mythological interpretation of environmental phenomena, but now, due to its misapplication, can only be considered, by rational human beings, as ludicrous in the context that it is generally accepted.

I refer you to the 1st chapter of Genesis in the King James version of the bible

"Gen 1:1 in the beginning god created the heaven and the earth.

Gen 1:2 and the earth was without form, and void; and darkness was upon the face of the deep. And the Spirit of god moved upon the face of the waters.

Gen 1:6 And god said, Let there be a firmament in the midst of the waters, and let it divide the waters from the waters.

Gen 1:7 And god made the firmament, and divided the waters which were under the firmament from the waters which were above the firmament: and it was so.

So here we have, according to the bible, a partial description of how the world was created. A rather fanciful tale, don't you think? I do not understand how any literate, rational mind could accept this story as an authentic, accurate, valid depiction of how the world began.

I will not spend a lot of time trying to tear down any illusion of the truth that might exist in the mind of some people, concerning these biblical passages that I have quoted above.

But, I seriously doubt that you are able to make intelligent sense out of the biblical verses herein quoted, **in a literal sense**.

Lets take a quick look at what is described in this yarn (a yarn when taken literally). --The earth is described as being without form and void. Now, for the sake of clarity, let us imagine that we are holding a baseball in the palm of our hand, stretched out before us. Let us imagine further that this ball is the planet earth.

Now, keeping in mind that this ball is our model, let us analyze the bible verses that we have quoted above. A partial quote says "And the earth was without form and void". Okay--now let us imagine that our ball has lost all form and not only that--it's void too, empty as a hollow ball. Can you do it; can you make *sense* out of this *nonsense*? Well, lets go further. The quote continues "and darkness was open the face of the deep, and the spirit of god moved upon the face of the waters:". Okay, don't take your eyes off the ball. The ball, in your hand, has no form and it's empty. Now! You must imagine that darkness is somehow on the face of the deep, of this shapeless empty ball. And not only that - but also, god's spirit has started moving on the face of the waters, located somewhere in or on this formless, empty, and deep ball (earth) that you are holding in your hand.

"And god said, let there be a Firmament in the midst of the waters, and let it divide the Waters from the Waters. And god made the Firmament and divided the Waters which were under the Firmament from the Waters where above the Firmament"

Can you do it! Is your imagination still working? Remember you must keep your eye on the ball in your hand that represents the earth. So now the sky (firmament) is created; it slides in between the waters that are situated in or on the ball in your hand that has no shape, is empty, with deepness and a floating god traveling over or perhaps on the waters, which (waters) are situated in or on the ball (earth) that has no form and nothing in it. **Is that clear enough for you?** Do you understand it? Or is it time for faith to arrive. Good old faith solves any and all questions. Because whether you understand a thing or not, - with faith, all things are possible, so they say.

My aim is not to bash or ridicule anyone's creed. But, it is a fact of life that most of us structure our religious beliefs not according to the dictates of our rational mind, but rather, in accordance with our hopeful hearts. And herein lies the problem-- is it better to have faith in this enigma, because it offers hope (even if only an illusion), *or should our evaluation be made on the basis of reason and pragmatism.*

As I wrote earlier, the laity's misguided literal concept of this myth was produced out of a misunderstanding of reality (our natural environment). Additionally, the effect of the myth was compounded by inculcating into the hearts and minds of the populace traditions and rituals established in devotion to the myths.

Biblical Plagiarisms

The first step, that we must take in order to uncover and discern the truth, apart from the confusedness caused by accepting these biblical verses as literally accurate, is to correctly identify the sources of this scripture.

Of course, there is no doubt as to who conveyed the biblical scriptures to the world, with the claim that they (the books of the bible) proceed from god, either directly or through his (gods) prophets; they are the Jewish people, Hebrews or Israelites if you like - the so called seed of Abraham. They, the Jews, were the first to claim that the bible or Pentateuch, the Torah, represent authentic history -and to portray god himself as the authority and source of this literature. The bible is not a book based on history but rather it is a book of symbolism. The tales of the bible fit into the same category as the ancient Greek and Roman myths. The bible can be rightly described as a book of Hebrew myths.

This is a very bold and self-righteous claim, made by those who claim to be god's only begotten nation i.e. by the Jewish people - that the old testament of the bible is derived from and authorized by god himself. They claim further that they as a race or creed are the chosen people of almighty god, his most loved, his favorite, the blessed seed of Abraham.

The Biggest Lie Ever Told, 4th Edition

We find the Jewish (Israelite) people first coming into biblical history, as an identifiable group, occurring approximately 4,000 years ago in the region, now known as Iraq, ancient Mesopotamia.

Their so-called *pact with god* begins with the mythical prophet Abraham, in the era beginning circa 2,000 BCE at the ancient city of Ur situated in Iraq, ancient Mesopotamia, the land between the two rivers (Tigris and Euphrates).

Nehemiah 9:7 through Nehemiah 9:9
[7]Thou art the LORD the god, who didst choose Abram, and broughtest him forth out of Ur of the Chaldees, and gavest him the name of Abraham; [8]And foundest his heart faithful before thee, and madest a covenant with him to give the land of the Canaanites, the Hittites, the Amorites, and the Perizzites, and the Jebusites, and the Girgashites, to give it, I say, to his seed, and hast performed thy words; for thou art righteous: [9]And didst see the affliction of our fathers in Egypt, and heardest their cry by the Red sea;

Genesis 17:1 through Genesis 17:8
[1]And when Abram was ninety years old and nine, the LORD appeared to Abram, and said unto him, I am the Almighty god; walk before me, and be thou perfect. [2]And I will make my covenant between me and thee, and will multiply thee exceedingly. [3]And Abram fell on his face: and god talked with him, saying,

[4]As for me, behold, my covenant is with thee, and thou shalt be a father of many nations. [5]Neither shall thy name any more be called Abram, but thy name shall be Abraham; for a father of many nations have I made thee.

⁶And I will make thee exceeding fruitful, and I will make nations of thee, and kings shall come out of thee.
⁷And I will establish my covenant between me and thee and thy seed after thee in their generations for an everlasting covenant, to be a god unto thee, and to thy seed after thee. ⁸And I will give unto thee, and to thy seed after thee, the land wherein thou art a stranger, all the land of Canaan, for an everlasting possession; and I will be their god.

So, 4,000 or so years ago, at Ur in ancient Babylon, conditions and circumstances warranted that the biblical Abraham gather his Family together and begin their migration toward the land of Palestine. That notable land of Canaan, described in the bible as the promised land of the Jews (Israelites).

Abraham is looked upon as the spiritual Father of the Monotheists. Jews, Christians and Muslims all view the mythical prophet Abraham, as their spiritual or religious father.
The foundation of Monotheism rest upon this so-called pact between god and Abraham, that is god says to Abraham: **worship me alone and I'll give you the world.**

Exodus 19:5
*⁵Now therefore, if ye will obey my voice indeed, and keep my covenant, then ye shall be **a peculiar treasure unto me above all people: for all the earth is mine:***

And herein, as expressed in these and many other verses in the bible, is *revealed* the **inborn Tyranny of Monotheism**; that it is not just a *religious* doctrine but a *political* doctrine that **seeks to dominate and exploit all** those that are not within its' ranks. The ultimate goal of the Monotheists (Jews, Christians and Muslims) is to proclaim and demand that we all submit to one god and one imperial government. **They even define the so-called Judgment Day as the day when their god will destroy all of us who dare to choose *free thought* over** religious and political tyranny. History confirms this.

So the concept of Monotheism is proclaimed to have begun with the covenant between god and Abraham. On a practical level, if Abraham was born and reared in the city of Ur, in Mesopotamia, he was undoubtedly influenced by the religion and history of that society.

Consequently, as Abraham began formulating his tenets, he of course borrowed from that storehouse of religion, philosophy and history that he was most familiar with, which, obviously, was Mesopotamian religion.

Actually, the bible version of creation is just one of many stories, or epics that Abraham and his successors borrowed from Mesopotamian Theology, for the purpose of making (formulating) their own religion - Judaism.

To prove this point, let of us now make some comparisons between Mesopotamian religion and the Torah/Bible of the Jews, Christians and Muslims.

Let us first review the biblical tale of Noah in Genesis of the bible. The following are quotes taken from the 6th the 7th and 8th chapter of Genesis:

Gen 6:5 And god saw that the wickedness of man was great in the earth, and that every imagination of the thoughts of his heart was only evil continually.

Gen 6:6 And it repented the LORD that he had made man on the earth, and it grieved him at his heart.

Gen 6:7 And the LORD said, I will destroy man whom I have created from the face of the earth; both man, and beast, and the creeping thing, and the fowls of the air; for it repenteth me that I have made them.

Gen 6:8 But Noah found grace in the eyes of the LORD."

Gen 6:13 And god said unto Noah, The end of all flesh is come before me; for the earth is filled with violence through them; and, behold, I will destroy them with the earth.

Gen 6:14 Make thee an ark of gopher wood; rooms shalt thou make in the ark, and shalt pitch it within and without with pitch

Gen 6:17 And, behold, I, even I, do bring a flood of waters upon the earth, to destroy all flesh, wherein is the breath of life, from under heaven; and every thing that is in the earth shall die.

Gen 6:18 But with thee will I establish my covenant; and thou shalt come into the ark, thou, and thy sons, and thy wife, and thy sons' wives with thee.

Gen 6:19 And of every living thing of all flesh, two of every sort shalt thou bring into the ark, to keep them alive with thee; they shall be male and female.

Gen 6:20 Of fowls after their kind, and of cattle after their kind, of every creeping thing of the earth after his kind, two of every sort shall come unto thee, to keep them alive.

Gen 6:21 And take thou unto thee of all food that is eaten, and thou shalt gather it to thee; and it shall be for food for thee, and for them.

Gen 6:22 Thus did Noah; according to all that god commanded him, so did he.

Gen 7:1 And the LORD said unto Noah, Come thou and all thy house into the ark; for thee have I seen righteous before me in this generation.

Gen 7:2 Of every clean beast thou shalt take to thee by sevens, the male and his female: and of beasts that are not clean by two, the male and his female.

Gen 7:3 Of fowls also of the air by sevens, the male and the female; to keep seed alive upon the face of all the earth.

Gen 7:4 For yet seven days, and I will cause it to rain upon the earth forty days and forty nights; and every living substance that I have made will I destroy from off the face of the earth.".

Gen 7:12 And the rain was upon the earth forty days and forty nights.

Gen 7:21 And all flesh died that moved upon the earth, both of fowl, and of cattle, and of beast, and of every creeping thing that creepeth upon the earth, and every man:

Gen 7:22 All in whose nostrils was the breath of life, of all that was in the dry land, died.

Gen 7:23 And every living substance was destroyed which was upon the face of the ground, both man, and cattle, and the creeping things, and the fowl of the heaven; and they were destroyed from the earth: and Noah only remained alive, and they that were with him in the ark.

Gen 8:3 And the waters returned from off the earth continually: and after the end of the hundred and fifty days the waters were abated.

Gen 8:4 And the ark rested in the seventh month, on the seventeenth day of the month, upon the mountains of Ararat.

Gen 8:6 And it came to pass at the end of forty days, that Noah opened the window of the ark which he had made:

Gen 8:7 And he sent forth a raven, which went forth to and fro, until the waters were dried up from off the earth.

Gen 8:8 Also he sent forth a dove from him, to see if the waters were abated from off the face of the ground;

Gen 8:9 But the dove found no rest for the sole of her foot, and she returned unto him into the ark, for the waters were on the face of the whole earth: then he put forth his hand, and took her, and pulled her in unto him into the ark.

Gen 8:10 And he stayed yet other seven days; and again he sent forth the dove out of the ark;

Gen 8:11 And the dove came in to him in the evening; and, lo, in her mouth was an olive leaf plucked off: so Noah knew that the waters were abated from off the earth.

Gen 8:12 And he stayed yet other seven days; and sent forth the dove; which returned not again unto him any more.

Gen 8:15 And god spake unto Noah, saying,

Gen 8:16 Go forth of the ark, thou, and thy wife, and thy sons, and thy sons' wives with thee.

Now that we have reviewed these bible references concerning the prophet Noah and his mission, it behooves us to make some comparisons to ancient Sumerian literature of a similar vain. After making these comparisons to Sumerian literature, which predates Jewish literature by centuries and in various cases, thousands of years; it becomes clear and obvious that the primary source for much of the Hebrew religious literature was undoubtedly Sumerian.

The Noah flood parallel is found recorded in ancient Sumerian literature within a poem, narrative known as "The Epic Of Gilgamesh."

The hero prophet of this epic was called Utnapishtim, by the Babylonians. I will here and now recount the ancient Sumerian Babylonian tale of Utnapishtim, and let you be the judge of whether or not the Hebrews copied and revised this story in the process of formulating their religious doctrine. The religion of the Sumerians was polytheistic, in that they worshipped or served various gods. They had gods that represented all the major aspects of life, such as air, water, the harvest, spring, fire, crops etc. etc. Even each city in the land had its on Patron god.

The story as recorded on clay tablets discovered at Nippur in southern Iraq (ancient Sumer) is summarized as follows:

In ancient times, their existed a city situated on the banks of the Euphrates River called Shurrupak. The gods became angry with the inhabitants of this city because of their loud riotous behavior. The clamor of these wild people was so incessant and over bearing that the gods could not get any sleep, because of the continuous noise. So the god Enlil (god of earth, wind, air) called the other gods to council concerning the problem. The gods deliberated on the matter and decided to destroy the city and its inhabitants with water (a flood). But one of the gods (Enki) had compassion for a citizen of the city, a man named Utnapishtim. So Enki (the god of sweet waters) decided to secretly warn Utnapishtim of the impending doom.

He, the god Enki, came to Utnapishtim in a dream, and warned him of the impending flood. He (Enki) told Utnapishtim to tear down his house and build a boat, and to take into the boat the seed of all living creatures.

The Biggest Lie Ever Told, 4th Edition

Utnapishtim obeyed his god and built the boat. It took him and his helpers 7 days to build it. After the boat was completed, the storms, torrential rains began. The tempest raged for six days and nights, non-stop. On the seventh day the storm ceased and calm returned.

Utnapishtim opened a hatch and peered out from his boat, all was water for as far as his eyes could see. His boat subsequently grounded on a mountain peak. The name of the mountain was Nicer. After being lodged (wedged) on the mount Nisir for seven days with still no sight of land, Utnapishtim loosed a dove, the dove flew away but returned, since it could not find land on which to rest. Then he loosed a swallow, which returned. Finally he loosed a raven, which did not return.

So this is the gist of the tale concerning Utnapishtim and the flood as recorded in the Epic of Gilgamesh.

Keep in mind also, that the clay tablets on which this epic was recorded are at least 5,000 years old and are written in a form that refers to an earlier time, long before the Hebrews came into history- (with the advent of Abraham) 4,000 years ago. So take your pick. Did the Hebrew, when *developing* their religion use this (The Epic of Gilgamesh) and other ancient literature as a reference? Or, are the similarities just coincidence?

At this point, why not take another example of Hebrew plagiarism concerning the prophet Moses- First the bible version of this prophet's birth; found in the second chapter of Exodus, of the bible:

Exeo 2:1 And there went a man of the house of Levi, and took to wife a daughter of Levi.
Exo 2:2 And the woman conceived, and bare a son: and when she saw him that he was a goodly child, she hid him three months.

Exo 2:3 And when she could not longer hide him, she took for him an ark of bulrushes, and daubed it with slime and with pitch, and put the child therein; and she laid it in the flags by the river's brink.

Exo 2:4 And his sister stood afar off, to wit what would be done to him.

Exo 2:5 And the daughter of Pharaoh came down to wash herself at the river; and her maidens walked along by the river's side; and when she saw the ark among the flags, she sent her maid to fetch it.

Exo 2:6 And when she had opened it, she saw the child: and, behold, the babe wept. And she had compassion on him, and said, This is one of the Hebrews' children.

Exo 2:7 Then said his sister to Pharaoh's daughter, Shall I go and call to thee a nurse of the Hebrew women, that she may nurse the child for thee?

Exo 2:8 And Pharaoh's daughter said to her, Go. And the maid went and called the child's mother.

Exo 2:9 And Pharaoh's daughter said unto her, Take this child away, and nurse it for me, and I will give thee thy wages. And the woman took the child, and nursed it.

Exo 2:10 And the child grew, and she brought him unto Pharaoh's daughter, and he became her son. And she called his name Moses: and she said, Because I drew him out of the water.

Very interesting tale, don't you think? But for the sake of comparison, let's take a look at the birth history of a great Mesopotamian king (Sargon I). Sargon was a king in the area of Mesopotamia who preceded Moses by over 1,000 years. Some historians call him the First Empire Builder. He conquered and ruled the entire area of Mesopotamia sometime around 2500 BCE. Historically he is known as Sargon I the great-ruler of Sumer and Akkad. He reigned for over 50 years. Like most Kings of the distant past, he had his god connection. Here given, is his own description of his birth and infancy as historically recorded on clay tablets over 4,000 years ago; I repeat over 1,000 years before the alleged advent of the prophet Moses:

The Biggest Lie Ever Told, 4th Edition

"My mother, the princess, conceived me: in difficulty she brought me forth. She placed me in an ark of rushes, with bitumen my exit she sealed up. She launched me in the river which did not drown me. The river carried me to Akki, the water carrier, it brought me. Akki. The water- carrier, in tenderness of bowels, lifted me
."The similarity between this quote of Sargon I, and the bible reference to Moses in Exodus 2nd chapter Vs 1-10 is absolutely staggering. And since Sargon's legendary tale came first, we can rationally conclude that the Jewish priest used this story as a reference while compiling their theological legend of the prophet Moses.

I could go on and on making references to the parallels between Judaism and the Sumerian religious-political literature that the Jewish priest studied, copied and plagiarized while formulating their religion (Judaism). But that is not the purpose of this book.

My purpose, in writing this book, is to supply the reader with a workable method, a universal formula for deciphering the truth as to how modern theology (as we know it today) actually and truthfully developed. The evolution of religion can be clearly and precisely understood, when *we utilize pragmatic methods of deduction; based on logic, reason,* natural law, and human psychology; linked with a working knowledge of our planets geological, environmental, and secular history over the past 15,000 years.

The Five (5) points of our Formula are as follows: # 1-In the beginning there was a *Contentious Environment* (nascent societies surrounded by a hostile environment without a developed understanding of the causal forces of nature) which led to # 2-*Myth*, the fanciful creation (based on superstition) of gods and Demons as the Controllers of the Forces and Elements within their environment. To # 3- *Ritualism* - the establishment of rituals and sacrifices to appease or please their imagined deities and demons. To # 4- *Tradition* - which is the continued reverence of outmoded rituals and customs by a society where scientific knowledge has increased to the point that they should know better. Nevertheless the Laity tends to continue the superstitious practices anyway, because of a religious indoctrination cultivated over the millennia and habitually perpetuated. To #

5, *Modern Organized Religion* - The political, financial, religious leadership alliance, that finds it to their advantage to perpetuate the ignorance of the masses for purposes of control, organization, defense, aggression, and the accumulation and protection of their (leadership's) wealth.

Bible not literally true

The bible, for the most part, is not literally true; it is a book of fables and allegories. This, of course, also holds true for the Torah and Quran, as well as many other religious scriptures, but my focus is on the bible because the bible is the book that my readership is most familiar with. The bible does, in fact, contain some noteworthy moral and dietary instructions, as well as agricultural advice and calendar recommendations – but most of the books that make up the bible deal with esoteric symbolism covering various categories. Some unenlightened souls insist that the entire bible is literally true and divine – I find that amazing. These lost souls think that their beliefs in the most ridiculous and outlandish yarns contained in the bible are testimonies to their great faith, rather then evidences of profound asininity or benightedness. The bible cannot be literally true; this planet is five billion years old according to our scientific research, but the bible claims that the whole universe was created about 6,000 years ago. The bible describes the world as being flat, with the sun and other planets, and stars revolving around the earth. These mistakes of fact do not bear witness to the ignorance of god but rather to the ignorance of the intellectually primitive people that wrote the book or were responsible for the tutelage of the general public with their interpretations of information gleaned from the so-called divine scriptures. Of course some of the writers were very wise and enlightened composers of esoteric symbolism, but not all – some were literal believers, similar to the fundamentalist of our present era; people who unrelentingly believe in the sacredness of the divine Word, but lack an accurate understanding of the true import of the Word beyond its literal interpretations.

The Biggest Lie Ever Told, 4th Edition

Witness these tales from the bible i.e. from the mouth of god, according to those that insist the bible is a divine revelation from god almighty:

(1) According to the 10th chapter of the Book of Joshua, Joshua and his army were at war with the Amorites, and Joshua felt that he needed a little help; they were winning in battle against the Amorites but night time was approaching and Joshua feared that the Amorites would escape under the cover of darkness before he and his army had completed their victory, so he called upon Yahweh to aid him. Yahweh responded in glorious fashion; according to the bible, god stopped the sun and the moon in their courses, he (god) made the sun stand still for the greater part of a day so that the Israelites could complete the slaughter of their enemies -

Joshua 10:12 through Joshua 10:14
¹²*Then spake Joshua to the LORD in the day when the LORD delivered up the Amorites before the children of Israel, and he said in the sight of Israel, Sun, stand thou still upon Gibeon; and thou, Moon, in the valley of Ajalon.* ¹³*And the sun stood still, and the moon stayed, until the people had avenged themselves upon their enemies. Is not this written in the book of Jasher? So the sun stood still in the midst of heaven, and hasted not to go down about a whole day.* ¹⁴*And there was no day like that before it or after it, that the LORD hearkened unto the voice of a man: for the LORD fought for Israel.*

Think of that; the sun stood still for almost a whole day. That means that the earth stopped rotating on its axis; I can't begin to describe the idiocy of such a claim! Are we to believe this actually happened? The only reason that so-called intelligent people say they believe this fairy-tale is because it appears in the bible, and the bible is supposed to be the word of god; and therefore they think that when dealing with what they believe is divine, faith should overrule reason. It is this attitude of forced theological ignorance that now, today has the world topsy-turvy, lost and falling in a hole that has no bottom.

(2) According to the 3rd chapter of 1Kings, we have a story that is supposed to exemplify the Wisdom of Solomon. It is written that two women made opposing claims as to the maternity of an infant child, and they went before Solomon to have the matter adjudicated; Solomon's response was to order that the child be slain, and this episode, for reasons that I cannot comprehend, religionists claim is exemplary of the great wisdom of Solomon -

1 Kings 3:16 through 1 Kings 3:28

[16]*Then came there two women, that were harlots, unto the king, and stood before him.* [17]*And the one woman said, O my lord, I and this woman dwell in one house; and I was delivered of a child with her in the house.* [18]*And it came to pass the third day after that I was delivered, that this woman was delivered also: and we were together; there was no stranger with us in the house, save we two in the house.* [19]*And this woman's child died in the night; because she overlaid it.* [20]*And she arose at midnight, and took my son from beside me, while thine handmaid slept, and laid it in her bosom, and laid her dead child in my bosom.* [21]*And when I rose in the morning to give my child suck, behold, it was dead: but when I had considered it in the morning, behold, it was not my son, which I did bear.* [22]*And the other woman said, Nay; but the living is my son, and the dead is thy son. And this said, No; but the dead is thy son, and the living is my son. Thus they spake before the king.* [23]*Then said the king, The one saith, This is my son that liveth, and thy son is the dead: and the other saith, Nay; but thy son is the dead, and my son is the living.* [24]*And the king said, Bring me a sword. And they brought a sword before the king.* [25]*And the king said, Divide the living child in two, and give half to the one, and half to the other.* [26]*Then spake the woman whose the living child was unto the king, for her bowels yearned upon her son, and she said, O my lord, give her the living child, and in no wise slay it. But the other said, Let it be neither mine nor thine, but divide it.* [27]*Then the king answered and said, Give her the living child, and in no wise slay it: she is the mother thereof.* [28]*And all Israel heard of the judgment which the king had judged; and they feared the king: for they saw that the wisdom of God was in him, to do judgment.*

Now keep in mind, it was the custom of the ancient Semites, as is still the custom among some African, Arabian, Asian, and other cultures that periodically the tribal community would come before the Elders or Patriarchs to have matters of law, disputes, and customs adjudicated; a system similar to the Circuit Judge court that use to operate in *early* America. So here, according to the biblical rendition, two women had a custody dispute so they went before the king to have the matter arbitrated – and the king responded by ordering the murder of the child by cutting it in half and handing to each claimant a remnant of the carcass, and this they call wisdom! Some say that this is clear allegory, **but nowhere in the biblical passages is this referred to as allegory; it is portrayed within the scriptures as historical fact,** so why do some say it is allegory? *The reason that the tale is generally accepted as allegory is because the allegorical message is very elementary, and easy to understand* – plus the literal interpretation is absolutely monstrous. I agree that the tale is allegorical but the point that I am making is that the bible is replete with allegory of this type whose definitions, unlike the Solomon story, are very arcane and obscure, hence we take many passages as fact because we don't understand the hidden meanings, and therefore assume that the writings are literally true, and this we do to our own spiritual detriment. The vast majority of the bible is pure symbolism, but not religious symbolism; it is astronomical, agricultural, cultural, and environmental symbolism. I give detailed explanations of this symbolism in some of my other writings; that is not the focus of this book.

(3) According to the 1ˢᵗ and 2ⁿᵈ chapter of the Book of Jonah, Jonah was given a mission to warn the city of Nineveh because of god's anger. Jonah sought to avoid the mission by fleeing to another locale. He took passage on a ship that was subsequently caught up in a storm, he eventually ended up in the sea, and was swallowed by a big fish and allegedly lived within the belly of the fish for three days. This story is portrayed in the bible as an historical event -

Jonah 1:1 through Jonah 1:6
¹Now the word of the LORD came unto Jonah the son of Amittai, saying, ²Arise, go to Nineveh, that great city, and cry against it; for their wickedness is come up before me. ³But Jonah rose up to flee unto Tarshish from the presence of the LORD, and went down to Joppa; and he found a ship going to Tarshish: so he paid the fare thereof, and went down into it, to go with them unto Tarshish from the presence of the LORD.

The Biggest Lie Ever Told, 4th Edition

⁴*But the LORD sent out a great wind into the sea, and there was a mighty tempest in the sea, so that the ship was like to be broken. ⁵Then the mariners were afraid, and cried every man unto his god, and cast forth the wares that were in the ship into the sea, to lighten it of them. But Jonah was gone down into the sides of the ship; and he lay, and was fast asleep. ⁶So the shipmaster came to him, and said unto him, What meanest thou, O sleeper? arise, call upon thy God, if so be that God will think upon us, that we perish not.*

Jonah 1:11
¹¹*Then said they unto him, What shall we do unto thee, that the sea may be calm unto us? for the sea wrought, and was tempestuous.*

Jonah 1:15 through Jonah 1:17
¹⁵*So they took up Jonah, and cast him forth into the sea: and the sea ceased from her raging. ¹⁶Then the men feared the LORD exceedingly, and offered a sacrifice unto the LORD, and made vows.*

¹⁷*Now the LORD had prepared a great fish to swallow up Jonah. And Jonah was in the belly of the fish three days and three nights.*

Jonah 2:1 through Jonah 2:2
¹*Then Jonah prayed unto the LORD his God out of the fish's belly, ²And said, I cried by reason of mine affliction unto the LORD, and he heard me; out of the belly of hell cried I, and thou heardest my voice.*

Jonah 2:10
¹⁰*And the LORD spake unto the fish, and it vomited out Jonah upon the dry land.*

Again, this tale is given in the bible as a historical event; no mention is made of it being an allegory, but common sense tells most of us that it must be allegorical because literally it does not appear rational. There are fundamentalists who will swear that this really happened and that belief is required as a matter of faith. This seems so inane, so why do some religionists insist that every word of the bible is literally true? The bible is indeed saturated with little tales (lies) that absolutely cannot be literally true, but the religionists feel that they must defend these little lies as literal truth at all cost, because they know that if they ever admit that the small lies (tales) are allegorical (although depicted in the Bible and Quran as historical), they open themselves up to a challenge from the realists that the biggest lie of them all (even though given in the bible as historical) must also be allegorical. The biggest lie of them all is that Jesus Christ rose from the dead. The tale of the resurrection of Christ fits into the same category as the other biblical tales given above. That tale of Christ rising from the dead after three days in the grave makes no more sense than Jonah living in the belly of a fish for three days. **But the Christian monotheists know that they must never compromise on the literal interpretation of the resurrection of Christ,** because to do so would undercut the very foundation of their form of monotheism. Witness biblical quote:

1 Corinthians 15:12 through 1 Corinthians 15:18

¹²*Now if Christ be preached that he rose from the dead, how say some among you that there is no resurrection of the dead?* ¹³*But if there be no resurrection of the dead, then is Christ not risen:* ¹⁴*And if Christ be not risen, then is our preaching vain, and your faith is also vain.* ¹⁵*Yea, and we are found false witnesses of God; because we have testified of God that he raised up Christ: whom he raised not up, if so be that the dead rise not.* ¹⁶*For if the dead rise not, then is not Christ raised:* ¹⁷*And if Christ be not raised, your faith is vain; ye are yet in your sins.* ¹⁸*Then they also which are fallen asleep in Christ are perished.*

And not only does the bible allege that Christ rose from the dead, but perhaps hundreds or thousands of others rose also from their graves concurrently with Christ, according to verses found in Matthew of the bible; Witness quote from my book "The Astrological Foundation Of the Christ Myth":

*"In fact, according to the bible, there was a multitude, perhaps hundreds , if not thousands , that were alleged to have been resurrected with Christ. **See the following verses,***

>*Mat 27:50 Jesus, when he had cried again with a loud voice, yielded up the ghost.*
>
>*Mat 27:51 And, behold, the veil of the temple was rent in twain from the top to the bottom; and the earth did quake, and the rocks rent;*
>
>*Mat 27:52 **And the graves were opened; and many bodies of the saints which slept arose,***

The Biggest Lie Ever Told, 4th Edition

Mat 27:53 **And came out of the graves after his resurrection, and went into the holy city, and appeared unto many.**

*Can you imagine All of these **walking Dead**, and there is not one smidgen of Secular history to confirm it. Two thousand years ago was not Pre-history. We have records of their politics, commerce, even inheritance and divorce matters, but nothing is mentioned, outside of the bible, about the stupendous event described in the biblical verses just quoted"*

Boy oh boy, I think that it would take an enormous, unimaginable amount of faith for most level headed people to accept the biblical verses quoted above as literal truth. We are told by Matthew that at the time of Jesus' resurrection, dead people in the local graveyards ascended from their graves, and dwelled among the living! Think of it, dead people rising up from beneath their tombstones, going into the city as witnesses to the resurrection of Christ – this according to god's so-called Holy Bible. I just wonder how all these dead people were dressed, and what about their physical appearance, their skin, eyes, etc – and what happened after their witnessing, did they go back into their graves or maybe perhaps they flew to heaven like Jesus. According to the bible, Jesus, after the resurrection and showing himself to the faithful, rode a cloud into the heavens:

Acts 1:9 through Acts 1:11

9And when he had spoken these things, while they beheld, he was taken up; and a cloud received him out of their sight. 10And while they looked stedfastly toward heaven as he went up, behold, two men stood by them in white apparel; 11Which also said, Ye men of Galilee, why stand ye gazing up into heaven? this same Jesus, which is taken up from you into heaven, shall so come in like manner as ye have seen him go into heaven.

So he left in the clouds, and he is prophesied to return in the clouds. I assume that heaven must be billions of light-years away and here we have Jesus traveling through outer space on a cloud, and maybe all of those graveyard escapees went to, but just weren't mentioned.

This is, so, so nonsensical. This tale is an insult to our intelligence, and is blatantly absurd. The only truth that can be found in the biblical verses quoted above is allegorical truth, period. I must mention also that the *prophet* accomplished a feat similar to that assigned to Jesus. According to Islamic lore, the prophet, along with the angel Gabriel, is alleged to have flown from earth, through heaven, on a winged horse, called Al Baraq, he met with Moses, exchanged greetings and conversation, continued his flight to another earthly location, and returned to his original point of departure – all in one night. This is mentioned in the 17ᵗʰ Sura of the Quran. **It must be understood:** either the scriptures (i.e. alleged revelations from god) are holy and the complete words of god, or they are *not* holy and *not* the complete words of god, period. The books cannot be partially holy, no more than women can be partially pregnant. If any part of the scriptures are open to question as to whether it is fable or literal, than the complete scriptures must, by all rules of common sense, be subject to the same critique – including the story of Jesus Christ. **These are facts** that we must deal with *rationally* and *dispassionately*, if we *sincerely* want to find the truth.

Chapter Five: The Resurrection Myth

In this chapter we shall explore the true symbolism of the Resurrection Myth, the myth of the resurrection of Jesus Christ.

According to this myth, Christ and two thieves were crucified on three (3) crosses,

Math. 27:38 "Then were there two thieves crucified with him, one on the right hand, and another on the left."

He suffers under darkness for three (3) hours, before crying out to his god;

*Math 27:45 "Now from the **sixth** hour there was darkness over all the land unto the **ninth** hour."*

He also laid in a grave, dead for three (3) days, before being resurrected and eventually ascending to heaven.

Let us review some other pertinent bible verses

Mat 16:21 From that time forth began Jesus to show unto his disciples, how that he must go unto Jerusalem, and suffer many things of the elders and chief priests and scribes, and be killed, and be raised again the third day.

Mark 8:31 And he began to teach them, that the Son of man must suffer many things, and be rejected of the elders, and of the chief priests, and scribes, and be killed, and after three days rise again.

Luke 9:22 Saying, The Son of man must suffer many things, and be rejected of the elders and chief priests and scribes, and be slain, and be raised the third day.

Mat 12:40 For as Jonas was three days and three nights in the whale's belly; so shall the Son of man be three days and three nights in the heart of the earth.

The essential and vital factor that will bring us to the correct interpretation of the resurrection myth, is *the number 3*. This number 3 is the key to unveiling the truth. Take notice of the emphasis placed by the authors of this scripture, on this number 3.

THE RESURRECTION MYTH

The Biggest Lie Ever Told, 4th Edition

Matthew 27:38 tells us that there were three (3) crosses. Matthew 27:45-46 tells us that the Christ suffered three (3) hours before dying. The other verses reiterate the point that the Christ must lay dead in a grave for three (3) days. And Math 12:40 even compares the story of Jonah in the belly of a fish, for three (3) days, as a prototype to Christ being buried for three (3) days.

The basis and method of our premise for deciphering how religious fallacy developed, is to trace the fallacy back to its *environmental* origin.
I have compared religious fallacies to legends. In the same or similar ways that legends (which may resemble actual history) originated from some actual historical events, so also have fallacies (religious myths) originated from the allegorical representations of reality (i.e. the symbolical, mythical renderings of seasonal, agricultural, and astronomical phenomena).

The further we distance ourselves from a thing, whether in time or space, the more difficult it becomes to identify it accurately. This is a universal truth. Therefore, in order for us, to bridge this gap of time and space, we must, somehow, go back to the beginning---the starting point. We can't do this physically. The only way that we can travel back in time is through *historical research*. We must adjust our thinking so as to relate empathetically with the minds of those people who first constructed the myths (ideas and rituals) from which our religious concepts evolved. **Mythology is the allegorical depiction of environmental phenomena.**

Now, before we take this myth (Resurrection Myth) and retrace it back to its origin (i.e. the environmental episode that the myth symbolizes), I think it is best that we first briefly review the primary progressive stages of religious evolution, keeping in mind that our religious beliefs have evolved culturally over thousands of years, completely devoid of any divine intervention in the form of genuine prophets of god or godly revelations. It's a safe bet that the creator god of this unfathomable universe has never, in fact, revealed itself to some person or persons, and missioned same as his earthly

THE RESURRECTION MYTH

representatives – all such claims are bogus in my view. The process of religious evolution started in prehistory when primitive mankind was besieged by a *Contentious Environment,* without a developed understanding of the causal forces of their natural settings, which led to the fanciful, imaginative conceptualizations of mythical gods and demons as the controllers of the forces and elements within their environment; and this spawned *Ritualism,* that is, the establishment of rituals and sacrifices to appease or please their imagined deities and demons. The rituals, overtime became traditionalized - which is the continued reverence of outmoded rituals and customs by a society wherein scientific knowledge has increased to the point that they should know better; but nevertheless the laity tends to continue the superstitious practices anyway, because of cultural and/or religious indoctrination, cultivated over the millennia and habitually perpetuated. And finally, *Modern Organized Religion - the political, financial, religious leadership alliance, that finds it to their advantage to perpetuate the ignorance of the masses* for purposes of control, organization, defense, aggression, and the accumulation and protection of their (leadership's) wealth, pursuant, in accordance with their way of thinking, to a more durable and stable society.

Let us now commence our unraveling of the Resurrection Myth. The first point that must be understood is that it is absolutely impossible, for anyone to be physically dead for three days and then somehow come back to physical life. If you think so, why not ask your neighborhood undertaker about the condition of a corpse after three days.

Death is a natural law. If you break this law, you're dead. If you obey this law, you're dead. There is no getting around it. The best that you can hope for is to understand its purpose, and to understand your purpose. We are more capable of understanding reality fully, after we accept it.

The key point of our first premise is that in the beginning humanity confronted a *Contentious Environment* without an adequate understanding of what motivated or sustained (caused) the environment, and this lack of understanding caused them to imagine mythical deities (spirits) as the controllers of the environment. Later, as society developed intellectually, they began to personify their myths. For instance, mankind in his earliest stages feared the wind and made prayer and supplications directly to the wind (god). Subsequently he imagined that the wind was not actually god, but rather an instrument of god. He imagined god as some kind of being and/or spirit that controlled the wind. He imagined god to be an entity with traits similar to himself; a being subject to anger, love, hate, vengeance, greed, beauty, sexuality, and all the rest, just like him. So Man envisioned his mythical deities in the image of himself – with the same shortcomings, impulses and traits. And mankind *adopted methods designed to influence their mythical deities that were identical to methods devoted to earthly monarchs* i.e. humility (prayer) sacrifice (taxes) devotion (loyalty) etc. Jesus Christ represents a personification of the sun-god. In Jesus the *sun-god* became the Son of god.

We will now show that *the Son (god) and the sun (god) are one and the same.* A study of man and his environment, thousands of years ago, is essential to understanding how and why the sun god became the Son of god, the Christ.

Religion evolved from the rituals and traditions of nature and sun-god worshippers. The traditional customs and rituals were solidly ingrained into the mentality of our so-called pagan ancestors, to the point of no return. They (the laity) held unyieldingly firm to rituals and traditions that had been cultivated over years of superstition and misinterpretation. Rituals and traditions that were first established years earlier when their ancestors lived in caves and tree houses or crude huts; eating wild game, foraging the forest, hills and plains for whatever substances their bodies would accept or tolerate as a food. With unreasoning fear and foreboding of a seemingly fickle environment, which they did not understand. Under these oppressive conditions of fear, ignorance, and want, they did their best to find a god or savior to help them and to save them from their plight.

THE RESURRECTION MYTH

In these primitive conditions of ignorance, deprivation and fear, were spawned mankind's first imaginings of god. And, as would be expected, they took the shortest intellectual route possible to finding their god, which led to the worship of the elements of nature and the sun.

The daily life of primitive society was a constant struggle for survival - therefore when they sought god, they focused on those elements within their environment which had the greatest impact upon their existence. They needed light; warmth, water, food, shelter, clothing and a god that would help them attain these basics. It is easy to understand why primitive societies were inclined to the worship of nature gods, including the sun – it was because the natural elements held unequaled importance and relevance to their survival. Nature worship was inherent in all primitive belief (religious) systems.

Transition From Primitive Religion To Modern Religion

When Christianity evolved at the dawn of the Pisces era, the problem that faced the intellectual leadership (religious, political, financial alliance) of that time was How to elevate their society to a higher degree. They (the priesthood) could not break the influence and control that primitive nature worship exercised over the masses. So they decided to do the next best thing. They decided to convert (evolve or merge) idolatry into emerging modern Christian religion. They decided to transfer the old pagan customs (modified or renamed) into the new religion. In other words, they conceded to the populace the right to keep their old practices, and rituals, (for the most part) but they labeled the rituals with different names and new applications. They couldn't change the people, in terms of their ingrained customs and habits; so instead, they sought to change the appellations of the popular pagan deities. They changed the names and/or applications of what the people worshipped; and introduced modified reasons for the traditional practices, thereby continued and retained under a new Christian guise.

This brings us to the conversion of the solar sun-god into the Christ son of god, which is our present focus. Let us now explore the parallels between the pagan worship of the solar sun-god and the modern worship of the Son of god. Keeping in mind, that ancient or primordial society worshipped the sun because of their dependence on the sun, and their fear of losing it (the sun).

In review the actual celestial/terrestrial effect and activity of the sun and earth: The sun is the center of our solar system. The seasons of the year are determined by the attitude of the earth in respect to the sun, as the earth revolves around the sun, making one complete circuit every 365 ¼ days, which is one (1) year. The earth is spherical in shape and rotates on its axis. The earth rotates on its axis (sort of like a wheel rotates on an axle). It takes the planet 24 hours to complete one rotation, which is one day. The axis of the earth is tilted at 23 ½ degrees. The tilt of the earth always leans toward the same direction. This tilt causes the earth's axis, at different times of the year, to incline toward the sun (which is summer) or to point away from the sun (which is winter) or to have positions half way between the two extremes of summer and winter, which causes spring or fall type weather. This tilt of the earth as it revolves around the sun causes the declination of the sun to change (from north to south) with the seasons. The position of the sun is at its highest point (north) in the summer, when the earth's axis is directed toward the sun. The summer is a time of warmth, sprouting vegetation, greenery and thriving life in abundance. This holds true, because in the summer, the earth is positioned to receive the greatest amount of the suns light and radiation, and the daylight hours are longer. The position of the sun is at its lowest point (south) in the winter when the earth's north polar region is slanted away from the sun. The winter, of course is a time of retrenchment, the weather turns cold, there's snow and sleet, and the lakes and ponds become frozen. Vegetation won't grow, animal life decreases activity or migrates, and the daylight hours are shorter.

THE RESURRECTION MYTH

The Biggest Lie Ever Told, 4th Edition

Primitive man dreaded the onslaught of winter as the worst possible hell. Survival of primitive man, at any time of the year was an unending, overwhelming struggle, a battle against the odds. But when winter arrived, his plight, his struggle, his hell on earth was magnified a hundred fold.

The primordial masses did not understand the forces that caused winter, but they noticed that the winter weather followed the descent of the sun to its lowest point (23 1/2 degrees below the celestial equator) in the sky during the month of December. Therefore primitive society worshipped the sun, prayed to the sun, sacrificed *to* and *for* the sun. **At the onset of winter, they would cry and beg** the sun (by means of rituals and sacrifices), To rise from its low point (a position equated with winter's sufferings) back to its high point of summer (a time that primitive man relished for his survival) The seasons of the year start at exact times each and every year. These times are determined, as I explained earlier, by the attitude (position) of the earth, relative to the sun as it (earth) revolves around the sun.

Primitive man observed and recorded (kept track) of these dates, because his survival depended on his ability to make haste while the sun was high; and thereby be prepared, as much as possible, for the oppressive onslaught of winter, which followed the steadily decreasing declination of the sun towards the southern horizon.

The seasons of the year commence on the following dates each year: March 21 spring, June 22-summer, September 23-fall, December 22-winter.

The *key to the connection between the sun god and the Son of god is the number 3*. The bible is replete with verses stating that the major sign for identifying the Son of god is that he would lay in a grave for three (3) days and then be resurrected - *born again*.

Jesus Christ is the personification of the sun-god. If you searched from now till doom's day, you will not find any secular history of a person living 2,000 years ago, in Palestine, by the name of Jesus Christ, that accomplished the feats that are attributed to him in the bible. The source of all knowledge concerning a person (prophet) called the Christ or Jesus are the biblical scriptures and other literature that was derived from the original biblical sources. Furthermore the bible was compiled and translated and revised by proponents of the Christian faith who established that religion, during the early centuries of this era (this era began approximately 2,000 years ago).

The idolaters or nature worshipers practiced a variety of pagan rituals that culminated each year, at the dawning of the winter type weather, on Dec. 25. They celebrated this day as the day of the Birth or Resurrection of the sun god. The sun was symbolized as a god under many different titles within many different cultures, Egyptian, Greek, Roman, and Aztec etc. They actually looked upon Dec. 25 as the day when the sun was born anew- resurrected into new life. This ritual worship of the resurrection (birth) of the sun-god on Dec. 25 goes back thousands of years into pre-history.

The primary, motivating factor that inspired early man to worship god, was his fear and dread of the potential fierceness of his environment. His (primitive man) major impetus to worshipping and sacrificing (sacrificial rituals) to the sun god was to assure that the sun god would continue protecting mankind from the ravages of the dreaded winter.

So for primitive man, the inception of winter, *December 22*, was the worst day of every year for him. **This day** (*December 22,* the start of winter) marked the beginning of the worst stage of his yearly struggle for survival. **This day** (*December 22,* the start of winter) was the harbinger of his potential perdition.
This day *December 22*, is referred to by astronomers as the Winter Solstice. This word "solstice", according to our dictionaries, means to *stand still, pause, a turning point.*

On *December 22* of each year, the sun reached its Winter Solstice, the lowest point of trajectory (angle of rays) of the entire year. After *December*

22 (the turning point), the sun again rises northward, which is a sign that summer shall come again!

Even though *December 22* marks the beginning of winter. And the weather turns progressively worst from that point (*December 22*) until the start of spring (March 21), all is not lost. Because the fact that the angle of sun's rays projecting on the earth, was moving progressively northward told early man that the warmth and comfort of the summer sun would eventually prevail. **But there was a period of doubt,** for early primitive civilization. Primitive man did not understand our universe and solar system as we do today. We, today, know exactly what causes the four seasons of the year. But early man did not. He did not possess knowledge of our solar system, the axis of the earth--its rotation and revolving around the sun. He did not understand that these forces operated by a natural, providential law that would stay its course, no matter what. Early man only understood the result, not the cause.

So each year, early society awaited the approach of *December 22*, with foreboding. *December 22*, the day of the Winter Solstice (definition is to stand still) was a day of reckoning for them. Because it seemed to them, as they observed and tracked the north to south movement of the sun, that on this day *December 22*, **the sun entered its grave.** The north to south progression of the sun can be likened to a swinging pendulum. You know that when a pendulum reaches its solstice (the point where it swings back - its turning point), that for a slight imperceptible moment, it actually stands still. But in terms of our vast solar system, **the point of solstice is not imperceptible. It lasts for days, three days to be exact.** For three days, after the sun reaches its solstice, it appears to stand still. This period of pause, between the sun's *descent* and a*scent*, wrought paralyzing dread and fear into the hearts and minds of our ancestors.

Over Time, they established rituals and traditions concerning this period (December 22 to December 25).

They passed the word through oral tradition, and eventually, after their societies established writing, wrote it down, concerning their sun god: *the*

THE RESURRECTION MYTH

sun shall lay in a grave (point of solstice) for 3 days. But after 3 days the sun shall rise, be resurrected, (according to Webster's dictionary, the word resurrect is linked to the word resurge, which means To Rise Again, to revive), and ascend toward heaven, (progressively ascend northward to the position of the summer sun). And when the sun completes its ascent upward toward the point of its summer solstice, it will comfort us and bless us with warm weather and long days and will save us (be a savior) from the ravages of winter.

So, this that I have explained to you here is the authentic true concept of the resurrection.[9]

When our ancestors spoke and wrote of the resurrection of the sun; they meant exactly that. It did not refer to a person, but to the solar sun. But, when the priesthood founded and established Christianity, they changed the sun to Son. The priesthood told the idolaters that the Son (Christ) was born on December 25, *just like their sun.* They told them that the Son had been dead in a grave for three days and then was resurrected (revived) and ascended to heaven (upward), *just like their sun.* The masses were unlettered, superstitious and dependent upon the leadership and guidance of the priesthood.

So the priesthood, with cunning and guile, made it easy for the laity to change religions without changing their ways (traditions). Consequently, the religious holidays of today are replete with traditions and rituals that are obviously of mythological origin. Our religions of today have been formed from the ashes of those (religions) of old; many customs that the monotheists think are unique to their various beliefs have been, in fact, practiced for thousands of years. **Witness the following quotes from the 1911 edition of the Encyclopedia Britannica,** in reference to the

---

[9]That is, in terms of the mentality and attitude of the people of that time and region. We must keep in mind, that throughout religious history, the priesthood has been aware of a Knowledge that transcends that possessed by the laity. This book does not address that esoteric knowledge. This book targets the laity, and I am focused on attitudes and conceptions in vogue amongst the laity.

THE RESURRECTION MYTH

similarities between an ancient Persian religion (Mithraism) and nascent Christianity:

"The most interesting aspect of Mithraism is its antagonism to Christianity. Both religions were of Oriental origin; they were propagated about the same time, and spread with equal rapidity on account of the same causes, viz. the unity of the political world and the debasement of its moral life. At the end of the znd century each had advanced to the farthest limits of the empire, ... and the struggle was the more obstinate because of the resemblances between the two religions, which were so numerous and so close as to be the subject of remark as early as the 2nd century, and the cause of mutual recrimination. The fraternal and democratic spirit of the first communities, and their humble origin; the

identification of the object of adoration with light and the Sun; the legends of the shepherds with their gifts and adoration, the flood, and the ark; the representation in art of the fiery chariot, the drawing of water from the rock; the use of bell and candle, holy water and the communion; the sanctification of Sunday and of the 25th of December; the insistence on moral conduct, the emphasis placed upon abstinence and self-control; the doctrine of heaven and hell, of primitive revelation, of the mediation of the Logos emanating from the divine, the atoning sacrifice, the constant warfare between good and evil and the final triumph of the former, the immortality of the soul, the last judgment, the resurrection of the flesh and the fiery destruction of the universe—are some of the resemblances which, whether real or only apparent, enabled Mithraism to prolong its resistance to Christianity. At their root lay a common Eastern origin rather than any borrowing. On the other hand, there were important contrasts between the two. Mithraism courted the favour of Roman paganism and combined monotheism with polytheism, while Christianity was uncompromising. The former as a consequence won large numbers of supporters who were drawn by the possibility it afforded of adopting an attractive faith which did not involve a rupture with the religion of Roman society, and consequently with the state. In the middle of the 3rd century Mithraism seemed on the

THE RESURRECTION MYTH

verge of becoming the universal religion. Its eminence, however, was so largely based upon dalliance with Roman society, its weakness so great in having only a mythical character, instead of a personality, as an object of adoration, and in excluding women from its privileges, that it fell rapidly before the assaults of Christianity. Manichaeism, which combined the adoration of Zoroaster and Christ, became the refuge of those supporters of Mithraism who were inclined to compromise, while many found the transition to orthodox Christianity easy because of its very resemblance to their old faith."

Chapter Six: Solar Symbolism, Festivals And Holidays

The Gospel, the Torah and the Quran as well as various other doctrinal books are not the literal truth. These religious books are based, in great part, on astronomical symbolism, allegory and myth. The myths of these scriptures fall into the same categories as the myths of ancient Rome and Greece. The stories within these books are, for the most part, allegorical representations of the movements of celestial entities within the cosmos and/or symbolical renderings of seasonal and agricultural transitions.

Much of the bible is based on solar mythology i.e. symbolism that reflects the movements of the sun throughout its annual cycle. Under this symbolism the sun is viewed as god; the constellations are viewed as locations through which the god (sun) travels. Of course in some cases the constellations are personified as prophets or deities, likewise with the planets and stars. These matters are covered in great detail in my series of books titled "The Astrological Foundation Of The Christ Myth".

So the sun (fire) is a mythological symbol of the divine, and darkness is the mythological symbol of the demonic forces or opponents of light (sun, fire). Witness this quote from my book, *The Astrological Foundation Of The Christ Myth, Book Two:*

Ancient Mythology was the rendering of scientific astronomy in a mythological format. Mythology symbolizes the movements of the heavenly bodies within the cosmos. Astronomy deals with charting the cycles of all the entities within the cosmos. The Prophecy that prevails in Mythology and religion is a result of this charting. **Of course a Prophecy**, *when delivered in a personified religious format, seems to be the miraculous foretelling of human events. But, in its Original form, the Prophecy did not pertain to future human activity. The Prophecy pertained to the future movements of celestial entities.*

Christ, The Sun And The Zodiac

Solar mythology is symbolism reflective of the sun's movement throughout its annual cycle. This system is very ancient, in fact we don't have a record of its absolute origin. It has existed in some form on all continents, in all ages. The ancients did not use scientific names to identify the cosmic entities; they used earthly names, they named the stars, planets, sun, moon, and constellations in duplication of the entities within their earthly environment. This is clearly exemplified in Greek and Roman mythology, which we all are familiar with, whereas the interplay between the cosmic lights are likened unto contending gods, such as Zeus, Hera, Aphrodite, Persephone, Hades, Demeter, Jupiter, Saturn, Diana, Venus, Ceres, Hermes, and many others. These names reflect cosmic stars, planets, and constellations that were personified in Greek and Roman mythology – their stories read like human intrigues but we all know the true references are to the cosmic lights.

All cultures have their forms of mythology, that is to say allegorical symbolism reflective of astronomy, agriculture, history, culture, and so on. Cosmic mythology existed among the Chinese, Hindus, Egyptians, Babylonians, Aztecs, Japanese, Irish, and many, many others, including the Hebrews. The biblical stories of the Old Testament and the New Testament are not historical, but rather are tales reflective of Hebrew mythology.

The biblical story of Christ is not historical; it is a tale of Hebrew mythology. Actually the Christ story is a mixture of Hebrew and Greek influences, descended from more ancient mythologies, but how we designate it, rather Hebrew or Greek or even Egyptian is not important because all of the ancient mythologies paralleled each other – they all told the same stories of the interactions of the cosmic lights under various cultural formats. Jesus was the sun, born on December 25th; under the allegorical symbolism incorporated by the early Hebrew or Hebrew-Christian mythologists. A human Jesus never lived, not under the name Jesus, or a name such as Jehoshua Ben Pandera or any other name – Jesus Christ never existed, period! The Christ story within the bible is an allegorical tale, just like the Greek stories of Zeus or Roman stories of Jupiter; anthropomorphic tales reflective of astronomical phenomena.

A clear example of Hebrew mythology reflective of astronomical phenomena is found in the biblical passages concerning the so-called angel "Lucifer". We all know that the term Lucifer (Latin: Light-bearing) refers to the planet Venus, according to our dictionaries. Venus is known as the Morning Star and also the Evening Star, as it plays both roles in the course of its orbit. When in its cycle as the Morning Star, it heralds the dawning of the sun; it shines at dawn as the brightest light in the sky, as if to challenge the sun. But when the sun breaches the horizon, it obliterates its (Lucifer's) light and sends it into oblivion (darkness). This astronomical event is described in Isaiah of the bible – take note as to how the writers have completely personified the planet Venus as the rebellious angel Lucifer in describing its interaction with the sun at dawn:

Isaiah 14:11 through Isaiah 14:19

¹¹Thy pomp is brought down to the grave, and the noise of thy viols: the worm is spread under thee, and the worms cover thee. ¹²How art thou fallen from heaven, O Lucifer, son of the morning! how art thou cut down to the ground, which didst weaken the nations! ¹³For thou hast said in thine heart, I will ascend into heaven, I will exalt my throne above the stars of God: I will sit also upon the mount of the congregation, in the sides of the north: ¹⁴I will ascend above the heights of the clouds; I will be like the most High. ¹⁵Yet thou shalt be brought down to hell, to the sides of the pit. ¹⁶They that see thee shall narrowly look upon thee, and consider thee, saying, Is this the man that made the earth to tremble, that did shake kingdoms; ¹⁷That made the world as a wilderness, and destroyed the cities thereof; that opened not the house of his prisoners? ¹⁸All the kings of the nations, even all of them, lie in glory, every one in his own house. ¹⁹But thou art cast out of thy grave like an abominable branch, and as the raiment of those that are slain, thrust through with a sword, that go down to the stones of the pit; as a carcase trodden under feet. This is pure allegorical poetry, written in a fashion that parallels the mythological writings of the Greeks and the Romans. Of course theologians will try to apply these verses to the unseen demon, Satan, or to a wicked Babylonian king perhaps, but if you diligently examine the phrases you will see clearly that the above is a personified description of cosmic interactions, planetary interactions between the sun and Venus as viewed from earth.

The biblical story of Jesus' life, from birth to death, is symbolic of the path of the sun through the Zodiac in the course of one year; his birth life and death are written in the stars. His story is a myth styled after the patterns of the ancient Greeks, Romans, Egyptians, and others. As the story goes, he was born in a stable on December 25th, placed in a manger, while the Shepherds were attending their flocks – this is patently true under the allegorical symbolism of the sun. The birth of the sun takes place in the sector of Capricorn; included within this sector are the constellations Cepheus (The King), Cygnus (The Swan), Delphinus (The Dolphin), Pegasus (The Winged Horse), and Equllus (The Small Horse). Within the Constellation of the king (Cepheus), there are two stars of note, among others that make up this constellation – they are Errai, and Alfirk; Errai means shepherd and Alfirk means flock, this explains the shepherds and the flock that were nearby at the time of Christ's (sun's) birth. Also, Christ was said to have been laid in a manger at birth – it so happens that when the sun is in Capricorn, at midnight, the stars that light the night sky at the *zenith* are of the sign *opposite* the sun sign[10], which in this case points to Cancer. Within the sector of Cancer, there is an asterism known as the Beehive; Beehive is a recent name, anciently this asterism was called the "Manger", clearly indicating the manger assigned to the birth of Jesus (the sun-god).

Actually, according to the *solar* symbolism, the sun (Christ) dies, and is born in the same sign (Capricorn) – that is the completion of a one-year cycle. I explained the death of the sun (Christ) earlier in the book as occurring on December 22, three days before its rebirth as the new Christ (sun) – now witness this excerpt from my book "The Astrological Foundation Of The Christ Myth" which explains one phase of the symbolism of the dying sun (Christ):

"Golgotha is the location of the crucifixion and as such represents the

---

[10] We are able to locate the sign that the sun is in by sighting the constellation that strides the midnight meridian, because midnight for the observer is high noon for the sun, 180 degrees from the coordinates of the meridian at midnight.

The Biggest Lie Ever Told, 4th Edition

Winter solstice. The word Golgotha and Capricorn share the same definition, as a term that refers to Skulls, Death. The Winter Solstice is symbolized by the terms Golgotha, Capricorn, Hades, Pit, Calvary, Hell, Bottomless Pit, Cave, Grave, Graveyard and other terms.

As explained earlier, the three days that Christ spent in the Grave refer to the three days period of Solstice. The sun, after it reaches its lowest point of declination, on December 22, Hesitates in Place for three days, before re-ascending northward toward the vernal equinox. The priest symbolized this three day period of solstice as being buried in the Grave for three days.

The Crucifixion of Christ, On The Cross, refers to the Cross in the Constellation of Cygnus(the Swan)' which lies in the same sector with Capricorn.

*The Two Thieves that are crucified with the Savior(Sun) refer to the Equinoxes. The one on the Right Hand is the Vernal Equinox. The one on the Left Hand(who bad mouthed the savior) is the Autumnal Equinox. The Equinoxes are referred to as thieves, because they are thieves of time. **They steal Time from each other**. When the Sun intersects either equinox, <u>for that day of crossing</u>, Time(Daytime and Nighttime) on the planet is brought into equilibrium, at twelve hours. **We have twelve hours of light and twelve hours of darkness, on the day of the Equinox**. In the case of the Vernal Equinox(which represents light), **He**, on the second day after the sun's crossing, **Steals Time** from the Autumnal Equinox(which represents darkness) and from this point, the world continues to have more light(daytime) than darkness, until the Sun crosses the Autumnal Equinox. **When the Sun crosses the Autumnal Equinox**, this thief(autumnal equinox) repeats the crime(theft of time) in the favor of increased Darkness."*

At the next cardinal point, the vernal equinox, Christ, the sun, is tempted or tried by Satan for forty days; See excerpt from my book "The Astrological Foundation Of The Christ Myth" that explains this symbolism:

"The Magnificent Forty:

Solar Symbolism, Festivals And Holidays

The Biggest Lie Ever Told, 4th Edition

The Number forty is one of the most significant symbolisms used within the scriptures. In consequence of this fact, I have inserted several _quotations from the bible , that give reference to the number forty(40). The number forty represents pure symbolism and allegorically expresses the interval of time between the sun reaching certain celestial coordinates(the equinoxes), and its(sun's) tangible effect upon the climate of our planet, after reaching those coordinates. The interval is forty days, even though the biblical editors may use weeks, or years, or hours, in the text, according to the subject matter of the tale , so that the unit(description) used will fit the context of the specific fable.

The interval is always referred to as a Struggle of some sort, some type of deprivation, or trial, or test. This is because of the extreme difficulty our solar sun experiences in vanquishing the winter cold from our atmosphere. After six months under the equator, the sun is now in position , when it reaches the vernal equinox on March 21, to restore warmth and moisture to the northern regions. But the victory of warmth over cold is not immediate, but rather a tug of war , back and forth, between the forces of light(warmth, salvation, reward and blessings) and darkness(cold, tempting devil, Satan).

But after 40 days(May Day), you can rest assured that the frost won't ruin your crops. The sun is now victorious, and free of the tempting(tugging) devil of winter.

> *Mark 1:9 And it came to pass in those days, that Jesus came from Nazareth of Galilee, and was baptized of John in Jordan.*
>
> *Mark 1:10 **And straightway coming up out of the water**, he saw the heavens opened, and the Spirit like a dove descending upon him:*
>
> *Mark 1:11 And there came a voice from heaven, saying, Thou art my beloved Son, in whom I am well pleased.*
>
> *Mark 1:12 **And immediately the Spirit driveth him into the wilderness**.*
>
> *Mark 1:13 **And he was there in the wilderness forty days**, tempted of Satan; and was with the wild beasts; and the angels ministered unto him.*

This Forty refers to the Lag Time between the Sun reaching the equinoxes, to the actual Terrestrial effect on the earth , that takes about 40 days to materialize. The

The Biggest Lie Ever Told, 4th Edition

Spring and the Fall begin officially when the Sun crosses the Equinoxes, but the effect on the earth's weather is delayed for a period of forty days.

This Period between the Sun's astronomical position and the earth's warming or cooling is a wilderness journey. The Goal or the Mount has been reached, but the effect on the earth's climate takes more time(40 days, which represents the amount of time needed for complete seasonal transition).

The Ancients symbolized this period in the Wilderness, by two semi-equinoctial holidays, namely May Day that comes forty days after the Spring equinox, and Halloween which comes forty days after the Fall equinox.

You will note that after the sun(under the type of Israel) crossed the Red Sea, it(sun-Israel) had to endure forty years struggle in the wilderness. And likewise, after Jesus(sun) crossed the sea(river of John The Baptist) he was immediately taken to task by the Devil for forty days of trials, temptation and fasting. The symbolism of the magnificent 40 is very explicit and occurs throughout the bible"

At the next cardinal point, the Summer Solstice, Christ (sun) enters Jerusalem, riding on two asses; see quotation from my book "The Astrological Foundation Of The Christ Myth" that explains this symbolism:

"Christ enters Jerusalem riding upon a Colt and an Ass

Mat 21:5 Tell ye the daughter of Sion, Behold, thy King cometh unto thee, meek, and sitting upon an ass, and a colt the foal of an ass.

Mat 21:6 And the disciples went, and did as Jesus commanded them,

Mat 21:7 And brought the ass, and the colt, and put on them their clothes, and they set him thereon.

Mat 21:8 And a very great multitude spread their garments in the way; others cut down branches from the trees, and strowed them in the way.

THE ASTRONOMICAL ANALOGY

Jerusalem is the Summer Solstice, the Apex, the highest point of the Sun's(Father's) travels. Ever since the Sun(Father) crossed the vernal equinox, His Focus has been on Jerusalem.

He(Sun) enters Jerusalem riding upon two asses. This refers to two prominent stars which the Sun rides(crosses) within the constellation of Cancer(the sign of the summer solstice). **The stars are** *Asellus Borealis* **(Northern Ass) and** *Asellus Australis* **(Southern Ass)."*

At the next cardinal point, Christ is betrayed, and captured by the underworld forces of opposition; he is tried and judged in court (Libra), and found guilty and sentenced to death, to the grave. The actual grave is at Capricorn as I have already indicated, but the capture that opens the pathway to the grave is at the autumnal equinox, at Libra, after September 22 when the sun crosses the Fall equinox. Libra (the 7th sign) was the sign of Christ's trial before Pontius Pilate as indicated by its sigil, the scales of justice (or *injustice* we might say). The gateways between the lower world and the upper world are at the equinoxes; the vernal equinox is the gateway to the higher hemisphere, equated with redemption, and the autumnal equinox is the gateway to the lower hemisphere, equated with suffering and death, according to the ancient symbolism. So when the sun falls below the equinox in the last part of the year and the earth approaches winter, the ancients saw that event as the imprisonment of the sun, or the wounding of the sun, whereas its light was impeded and made ineffective; the imprisonment of Christ and the eventual crucifixion of him is symbolic of the span from the autumnal equinox to the sun's death at the winter solstice, in the *annual phase* of the *solar* symbolism. Of course, biblically the resurrection of Christ takes place proximate to the vernal equinox; this is because of the cultural input from the Hebrew-Christians who wrote the biblical Christ myth. They fashioned the Christ after the sacrificial lamb of the Passover festival. It was the custom of the Jews to sacrifice lambs or goats proximate to the equinoxes, both vernal and autumnal; they also linked this sacrifice (killing of the animal) to the *expiation of their sins* – the animal was termed a scapegoat, a scapegoat that carried the load of punishment for the accumulated sins of the Jewish population. **This is where the myth comes from that Jesus died for the sins of the world;** it's simply a copy of the old pagan, superstitious customs of the nomadic Hebrews. The bible clearly calls Jesus the Passover, that he was a substitute for the lamb of the Jews brought forth to human form under the Christian doctrine, which (doctrine) was composed by the early Christians who were actually Jews, members of a Jewish sect that later, overtime became distinct as Christians.

The Biggest Lie Ever Told, 4th Edition

Correlations Between Biblical Names And Astronomical Entities

Since the histories within the bible are actually fables, it follows also that the names of various prophets and locations given therein are not actual people or locales; but rather these *names are symbolical titles* and descriptions of cosmic entities, actions, elements and/or cycles. We are better able to comprehend the mythical symbolism when we possess an accurate understanding of the various titles (names) used in the bible. The following short list will aid us in that effort and help to exemplify my point.

I have used various Dictionaries and Encyclopedias as research sources in the compiling of these definitions; and I have, of course, integrated my concepts as a guide to understanding the Gnostic symbolism contained within these terms.

Witness on the following pages the titles (names) that clearly show their cosmic and/or environmental connection:

Solar Symbolism, Festivals And Holidays

Title	Definition	Comments
Adam	Red, Dust, Earth, Ruddy	Mythically, the term Red often refers to the cosmic region beneath the equinoxes commencing at the Autumnal equinox, also red earth which may indicate the desert in the environmental symbolism
Eve	Life, Enliven	Eve was created from the essence of Adam, so the possible seminal connection between earth and sprouting life is quite evident
Cain	Farmer	
Abel	Shepherd	
Terah	Father of Abram (Abraham), Place in Desert, Goat, Capra	The astrological sign Capricorn refers to the Goat, also called Azazel, and a desert location. Abraham was the son of the goat. Capricorn is the birthplace of the sun on December 22 (25). See *The Astrological Foundation Of The Christ Myth Book Three* for details.
Ur	Birthplace of Abraham. Light, Fire, Valley, Fire oven, Flame, Moon City	City dedicated to the moon god Sin (Sinai). Sin was a Babylonian Moon god whose worship was centered at Ur (Definition is Fire, Flame = sun). This was the birthplace of Abraham

Title	Definition	Comments
Abram	Exalted Father	In mythology the term *Father* often (if not always) refers to the sun. The term Father indicates Progenitor, Creator, god our Father, ruler, controller and that is the Status of the sun in our universe
Ab	Father	Hebrew term for father
Ra	sun	Egyptian name of sun god
Ham	Hot, Heat	Biblical definition of Ham is *Hot* which actually (mythologically) describes the intensity of the summer heat or tropical heat as apposed to the *lesser* heat of the winter season
Abraham	Father Of The Multitude	**Gen 17:1-6** states that god changed name of Abram to Abraham (at the age of 90 years) as a sign of god's covenant with Abraham to make him father (progenitor) of a multitude. **Mythologically** the covenant is when Abraham (sun) reached the vernal equinox (sign of the Ram) after rising 90 degrees (age of 90) from the sign of Capricorn. **At this point** the suns rays become a multitude i.e. intensified (hence adding the term Ham (hot heat) to the term Abram. So the term Abraham indicates the sun above the equinoxes while Abram is the sun below the celestial equator after its birth in Capricorn. *See my other writings for details.*

Title	Definition	Comments
Israel	god Prevails, Strives, Rules	The name of Jacob was changed to Israel after he wrestled and defeated a man (angel) in a battle that lasted all night and was ended at the break of dawn. He defeated his opponent by striking him in the Hollow of his thigh. This is found in **Genesis: 32: 24-30**. Mythologically, this clearly symbolizes the struggle of the sun against the forces of darkness. The *Hollow* of the thigh actually refers to the Loins, Groin, the generative factor. The *Phallus* is often used in mythology to indicate the equinoxes, often symbolized as a Steeple or Obelisk. When Jacob (like Abram) defeated the forces of darkness/nether world his name was change to Israel in recognition of his ascension into the realm of the Elect (above the equinoxes or Horizon). See my book – *The Astrological Foundation Of The Christ Myth* for details.
Samson	Of The sun, Sunlight, Ray, Brilliant	The story of Samson is in the 16ᵗʰ chapter of Judges. He clearly symbolizes the sun as the definition of his name indicates. He was captured and blinded after 7 locks of his hair were cut. The sun enters into the underworld in the 7ᵗʰ month of the Jewish religious year and its light is weakened in the declinations below the equinoxes, so the correlation is vivid. His strength returned and he destroyed his captors after

		his hair grew back (after completing 6 months in the underworld and reaching the vernal equinox)
Solomon	Peace, Quiet	The syllables of this name are intriguing: Sol is sun in Latin and Omon is strikingly similar to Amon, the Egyptian god.

Religious Holidays Are Pegged To The Annual Circuit Of The sun

Our religious holidays are geared to the cycles of the sun. All of the monotheistic religions, which primarily include Islam, Christianity and Judaism are mythological representations of the natural environment. The ancients fashioned their spiritual concepts as mythological copies of natural phenomena, the environment and its interactions. They pictured the sun as the ruler of the universe, the life giver, the conqueror of darkness and cold, the scorcher with its *intense* fire, the compassionate with its *soothing* heat. When the sun triumphantly appeared on the eastern horizon at the dawning of the day, the whole universe (from our earthly perspective) was seen bowing in submission to the greatest of all lights. All the stars and planets of the higher and lower heavens were vanquished without trace at the downing of the great sun god. This physical reality is the true seminal generator of our religious rituals in reference to an omnipotent conquering god, evolved from the customs of the ancients.

So when our ancestors developed customs and rituals within their spiritual systems, their *guiding* lights were the cosmic lights. They personified these lights as local and regional deities and they also imagined the environmental forces of nature as somehow infused with benevolent or malevolent spirits emanating from the great cosmos.

They formed their primitive religious philosophy in direct parallel to the material universe and accordingly the rituals and customs of the ancients were fashioned as duplications of the movements and interactions within the cosmos. Anthropologist may use the term *Imitative Magic* in describing this human phenomena - and they're on the mark in this case. Their rituals were symbolical imitations (mimicking) of celestial movements, interactions, and stations (cardinal points). The adherents believed that by imitating the perceived actions of their mythical deities through rituals, that they might magically achieve the same or similar benefices enjoyed by their deities. And also, as imitation is the greatest form of flattery, their rituals also served as a form of supplication to their mythical gods.

And within this mix were included symbolisms reflective of agricultural and pastoral activities that, of necessity, could only be successfully promulgated within specific seasonal constraints. These seasons were identified when certain celestial entities arrived at specified coordinates within the heavenly cosmos. Our modern religious customs have evolved from those primitive systems of the past.

Our focus is on the annual circuit of the sun and I will use the remaining pages of this chapter to exemplify correlations between our modern religious rituals and ancient sun and nature worship – the true basis of monotheism. We will trace the annual circuit of the sun and show that our modern religious holidays are, in fact, replications of the ritual festivals of the ancient sun (fire) and nature (environment) worshippers. Jesus Christ is a mythical representation of the sun.

Parallels Of Christian[11] And Pagan Ritualism

Carnival

Traditionally, this festival is a pre-Lenten observance of revelry and debauchery that is observed in the week or so preceding the rigors of Lent. The root meaning of the word *Carnival* is to take away meat. The adherents masquerade in hideous costumes and parade about in wild and frenetic glee. The centerpiece of this merrymaking is a huge grotesque effigy that is the

---

[11] My reference to Christian rituals applies equally to Islam and Judaism. All of the Monotheistic rituals are derived from the same core.

personification of the *Carnival* (gigantic puppet (he waves to the crowd) with big smiling face with rosy cheeks, top hat, oversized boots, gaily colored pants and jacket). This mock creature is, in the early phases of the festival, paraded through the town and applauded and praised, but in due course he is cursed - judged as guilty of crimes against humanity and executed.

Esoterically, The *Carnival* is a representation of Winter, the Demon of the Underworld. The Vernal Equinox is the place of judgment; it is the place of the final war between the forces of darkness and light, coldness and warmth. Spring begins when the sun crosses this point (vernal equinox) and winter is defeated. The ancients saw this point of intersection in the suns annual cycle as a battlefield, like unto Armageddon. Winter was seen (in the picturesque language of the ancients) as an oppressive demon that brought suffering and starvation to humanity, and springtime, on the contrary, as an avenging savior that defeated the demon and restored goodness to humanity. *The End Of The World* only means the *end of a cycle* and in this case that cycle is the *annual cycle of the sun* that is ended and also renewed at the vernal equinox, the point of *Judgment*. The merriment of the Carnival is analogous to the merriment referred to in the bible in Matthew: 24: 38 wherein Jesus indicates that in the Last Days there would be great gaiety and celebration before the final judgment.

Shrove Tuesday (Mardi Gras)

Traditionally, The last day of the pre-Lenten festival of *Carnival* and the day before Ash Wednesday, commencing the period of Lent. Shrove Tuesday is noted for wild frenetic merrymaking. The participants masquerade in various hideous costumes. The usual climax of Shrove Tuesday is the execution of the *personification* of the *Carnival* (a grotesque figure made of plaster or such and fashioned for the occasion) **in a bonfire**. Customarily a mock trial is held and the *Carnival* is **judged** for his sins/crimes against humanity – afterwards he is found guilty and executed by being **burned to ashes**.

Esoterically, This day of Mardi Gras (Shrove Tuesday) carries the symbolism of the Judgment Day. On this day the Demon of the South is destroyed by Fire. Fire is the symbol of the sun; fire is the destructive power of the sun. It is with the power of fire that the sun is able to destroy winter and thereby restore warmth and moisture to our planet. Hence, casting the *Carnival* upon a pyre and burning him to ashes is a symbol of the destructive power of burning sun as it rises above the declination of the vernal equinox. The custom of setting bonfires upon the mountains and hills of various regions during the period preceding Lent and Lent itself was very wide spread a few years ago. The custom still exist (I am told) though not with the fervor of years ago. These bonfires were set in testament to the growing power of the conquering sun as it approached its glory at the vernal equinox. Read *The Golden Bough* by *Sir James Frazer* for details on this subject.

Ash Wednesday

Traditionally, The first day of Lent. The adherents receive a mark of ashes or their forehead as a sign of penitence.

Esoterically, this is the first day of Lent and the Fire (sun) worshippers are relishing their coming victory over the demons of winter. The coming victory was symbolized by the festival of the Carnival and his horrible execution. So now, in their glee and anticipation, the adherents scoop up the ashes of the Carnivals dead corpse and sprinkle the ashes upon their bodies or smear their forehead with the ashes; as a testament to the destructive power of the burning sun; that burns its enemies to ashes.

Lent

Traditionally, This is a forty-day period of Fasting and Penitence in imitation of Christ Fasting for forty days in the Wilderness.

Esoterically, this 40 day period of Lent is the last leg of the suns struggle to surmount the Mount of the equinox. The final stages of the war between the conquering sun and the winter demons (as the ancient expressed it) commences with Lent. Trace the meaning of the word Lent and we discover that it refers to the Lengthening of daylight as the sun approaches and surpasses the spring equinox.

Palm Sunday

Traditionally, The Sunday before Easter, commemorating the entry of Jesus into Jerusalem. Palm branches were spread out before him as he proceeded into the city.

Esoterically, Jesus is the sun - and the symbol of spreading palm leaves before his procession signifies the vivifying power of the sun. For as the sun conquers the winter as it passes through the Gates of the equinox, *it (sun) causes the earth to sprout with life and greenery* at its passing. So the palm leaves spread before Jesus was a symbol of this natural effect of the spring season.

Passover

Traditionally, This observance commemorates the Exodus of the Hebrews from bondage in Egypt.

Esoterically, Israel like Jesus is a symbol of the sun. The Israelites were never in bondage to the Egyptians in actual history – this is 100% myth. Israel is the major sun symbol of the Old Testament and Jesus is the major sun symbol of the New Testament. The true Exodus is the exodus of the sun from the southern hemisphere into the northern hemisphere, which is accomplished when the sun crosses the vernal equinox. I have given an extensive explanation of this in *The Astrological Foundation Of The Christ Myth Book Two*.

Easter

Traditionally, This observance commemorates the resurrection of Jesus Christ.

Esoterically, Easter is the official beginning of Spring which is symbolized in today's culture by the dawning of new clothes, as a symbol the earth being clothed anew with the greenery of the new Spring season. The rabbit and the egg are also fertility symbols. The resurrection of Jesus from death symbolizes the resurrection of the sun from the death that it experienced when killed by the demons of winter, that is to say the effect of the winter weather in overcoming the power of the sun to warm the earth was seen as the death of the sun, in the picturesque language of the ancients.

Birthday Of John The Baptist

Traditionally, Commemorated on June 24

Esoterically, astrologically *John The Baptist* is a mirrored image of Jesus. The birth date of the mythical Jesus is on December 25, which is *3 days* after the Winter Solstice. *The mythical John was* born on June 24, which is *3 days* after the Summer Solstice. So the birthday of *John The Baptist,* at June 24, was placed so as to signal when the sun reaches the position of the Summer Solstice. This is covered extensively in *The Astrological Foundation Of the Christ Myth Book Three.*

Halloween (All Hallows Eve)

Traditionally, celebrated on October 31 on the eve of All Saints Day.

Esoterically, Halloween is placed so as to signal the final end of summer. The sun, at this point in the calendar, has been captured and chained by the demonic forces of the underworld (winter). The masquerading devils, ghost and demons of the Halloween festival are a signal that Satan (winter) reigns at this time of the year. Of course Fall actually starts when the sun crosses the autumnal equinox on September 22, but the ancients observed that the effect of winter was not immediate on that date. It takes *40 days* for winter (Satan) to wrestle the summer heat out of the sun and that takes us to October 31, Halloween.

Christmas

Traditionally, celebrated on December 25 as birthday of Christ

Esoterically, the sun is symbolically reborn on December 25 after lying in the grave of the solstice for three days. The solstice is on December 22 and this represents the death of the sun because it is the lowest declination of the sun at minus 23 ½ degrees below the celestial equator.

Baptism

Traditionally, a ritual that signifies purification and spiritual rebirth – an initiation required before the adherent can be admitted into heaven
Esoterically, the ritual of baptism mimics the annual circuit of the sun for the period it is beneath the equinoxes in the southern hemisphere. In one phase of the mythology, the ancients viewed the period of the suns passage below the celestial equator as a type of purgatory. Also in regards to the daily circuit of the sun – the ancients imagined that as the sun set on the western horizon it entered into the celestial waters of the underworld where it suffered many trials and tribulations. The effect of traversing these perilous celestial waters was purification, which was verified when the sun appeared anew and glorified at the next dawning day. The sun was imaged as a deity that was half man and half fish in one phase of the mythology, which was the god Ioannes.

Christian Eucharist

Traditionally, a sacrament in remembrance of the death of Jesus Christ, whereas bread is taken as his body and wine is taken as his blood.
Esoterically, the explanation for the Eucharist is found in the astrological sign of Virgo. Virgo, of course is the Virgin Mary and in her sign Virgo stands holding a stalk of wheat (bread). Virgo and her stalk of wheat is an esoteric precursor to the symbol of the Madonna and child. The stalk of wheat represents the child Jesus, hence the term *Bread Of Life* for his description. Also within the constellation of Virgo is the star Vindemiatrix – the definition of this term is Grape Gatherers. Of course grapes are the substance of which wine is made, hence wine is the symbolical blood of Jesus used for the Eucharist. This is not the only symbolism of the Eucharist.

Assumption Of The Virgin Mary

Traditionally, commemorated on August 15, as the date when the Virgin Mary rose from earth directly into heaven

Esoterically, the early church fathers claimed that the mythical Mary rose to heaven whole body and soul just like her mythical son Jesus. Since we know that Mary is symbolized by Virgo, this is easily explained. During the course of the suns annual cycle, all of the zodiac constellations are, in their turn, lost in the light of the sun. They seem to rise to the sun as the sun crosses over their positions. When the vernal equinox is in Aries, the sun crosses over Virgo in August in its annual circuit – so the Virgin Mary rising to heaven symbolizes the sun's transit of the zodiac sign of Virgo.

Chapter Seven: Insights On Fasting And Prayer

Prayer and Fasting are fundamental to all religions. The popular purpose of Prayer and Fasting is to communicate to and influence the deities. Those who are least capable of coping with the adversities of life are often the ones who seek godly intervention so as to improve their situations or to rescue them when in distress. This attitude is linked to the primordial superstitions of our ancestors, that is that nature and people are under the control of or possessed by spirits; and that these spirits can be influenced by personal sacrifices and prayers.

And of course, when we are overwhelmed by problems and tasks that may require solutions beyond our understanding or abilities, we may be stimulated to pray for godly assistance.

Some see prayer as a way of glorifying god or giving thanks for his mercy or blessings. This attitude reflects a belief in god as a monarch, a king to whom homage must be paid, or else.

I personally believe that fasting, faith and prayer[12] are essential to our spiritual (psychological) well being; and also, for the progressive moral and ethical development of our spiritual nature. Fasting and prayer may help reinforce and impress on our psyche certain values that we deem admirable. We humans have a spiritual nature as well as an instinctive carnal nature, and I believe that we need methods that help balance these apposing natures.

The above written is, to my way of thinking, a rational mature attitude concerning fasting and prayer. I'm sure you agree! But, there are many people who fail to share our attitude. They believe that by sincerely pleading with god (through fasting and prayer) they can extract from the almighty some Special Favor, of particular benefit to them. Favors that otherwise would not have occurred except by divine intervention, which

---

[12] Actually I prefer Meditation

was evoked by reason of their sincere solicitations (prayer) and sacrifice (fasting).

Some people have a faith that is so strong (misguided) and sincere (blind) that they believe god is just waiting around for an opportunity to grant their impassioned personal request. Sort of like a parent that gives into their children out of love and compassion. They believe that, even if they are caught in the midst of the worst possible calamity, such as an earthquake, hurricane, epidemic or whatever, that they can survive by reason of gods special blessing on those who have faith, and who exhibit their faith through intense supplication.

I am prompted to re-call a statement that I read as a child, concerning the alleged power of faith. A saying that I have never forgotten after 40 years: "*For those who believe, no proof is necessary---For those who don't believe, no proof is possible*".

I can't imagine living without faith, but faith must be anchored by reason, for if not so anchored, it (faith) becomes an illusion.

Nature's evidence indicates that god favors winners, not losers

You will agree with me, I'm sure, that the methods and actions of the people who dominate or are considered most progressive in this world are not guided by *unreasonable* faith in unseen and mysterious forces. They put faith in themselves and their own abilities. And their system seems to work to their benefit. As for Fate and Destiny, the very definitions of these terms indicate that we have no control to alter their course, so perhaps we are better off to live our lives as if we are in control; even though various factors tend to limit the control that we have over our lives.

The underdogs seem to think, that because of their position of inferiority (in terms of power and wealth) that they hold special favor with god. They have faith that one day god shall (compassionately) elevate them to positions of dominance, influence and authority. But why - for what reason would god show favor to the disadvantaged, the have-nots', the weak, the suffering and oppressed of humanity? Why should god turn against the progressive and industrious people of this world, who excel in intellect and achievement? Why should god join the ranks of the losers? There is no logical reason! *This attitude is an example of faith turned to illusion!*

I have not been able to find one instance in secular history where people were elevated from positions of disadvantage forward to positions of advantage or sustained dominance, except by their own efforts, qualifications, and persistence. Of course, favorable circumstances have often altered history to the advantage of some people. We might call these favorable circumstances good luck, or an answer to faith. But what benefit is there in favorable circumstances, if the blessed are not prepared to seize the opportunity of the day.

Those who live by faith alone are destined to live a life unimproved by time. If faith is your only beacon, then you can rest assured, that what you are today is all that you will ever be.
But, to get back to our point, concerning the origin of Fasting and Prayer within our religious systems. Within religion, there are prescribed times for fasting. First, let us define the word "Fasting", in *its* religious context. The following definition is pretty well on the mark:
To abstain from food and nourishment as a religious obligation; voluntarily for a specified period of time - inducing suffering on the body by overcoming one's appetites, or as a token of grief, or humiliation and penitence.

My encyclopedia describes **Fasting** under three Headings – *Magical*, *Ethical* and *Religious*. Depending on the motivation of the Faster, he or she may use the fast as a means of gaining ascendancy over nature by evoking powers that might not otherwise prevail in one's gluttonous state. People tend to believe that *fasting* strengthens their moral fiber, and endows them with greater moral character so as to resist life's varied temptations. Of course many believe that by voluntarily enduring the suffering and deprivation induced by the fast, they are proving their sincerity and devotion to a deity or cause of faith. This goes to the intent of the *fast* i.e. to the motivation of those who abstain for religious purposes.

The aforementioned explanations make two major points, among others: #1 the Fasters' intent is to influence nature (his environment) for his personal or community advantage. #2-The Fasters' intent is to convince god of his fidelity.

Now, let us examine two annual religious festivals that include fasting as a major component, to help us home in on how and why fasting developed into a religious tradition. Remember our formula! that in the beginning there was #1 Contentious Environment (a hostile environment which man did not understand) and this lack of understanding produced #2 Myth (a make-do explanation) which led to #3 Ritualism (methods of worshipping or serving the myth).

Fasting fits into item #3 of our formula i.e. ritualism. Fasting (in its original intent) was a pagan ritual used to serve and/or propitiate the mythical gods. Let us examine the "lent-Easter" of the Christians and the "Passover" of the Jews. Both of these events (Lent-Easter and Passover) are observed at proximate times each year. Passover commences about the 14th of the Jewish month of Nisan, which occurs near the spring equinox. The adherents fast for seven days (abstain from leavened bread). Easter is celebrated on the first Sunday after the full moon following the spring equinox. Easter is preceded by lent (40 days of *fasting*, in which the adherents significantly reduce their intake of food).

The point of prime significance concerning both of these festivals (Lent-Easter and Passover) is that they are inherently connected with the spring equinox, the date that marks the lengthening of daylight hours and consequently the approach of the crop (planting) season.

It is therefore, quite easy to recognize the possible intent or focus of the idolaters who practiced the Fasting custom[13]. Their desire was to influence the gods and/or forces of nature, in order to receive the blessings of a propitious growing season. As we discussed in earlier portions of this book, they felt that through sacrificial rites and self-punishments, they would evoke the mercy and blessings of god upon their seasonal efforts.

Of course, the Christian priesthood has concocted fallacious reasons, which they feed to the public as to why they should fast (religiously) at this and other times of the year. But the truth lies in history.

Concerning prayer, some of us look upon prayer as a way of praising our god, a form of flattery if you will. Through prayer, we inform god of how much we love him and appreciate him. Perhaps we think god is listening to our billions of prayers (the earth's population is around 5 Billion) and keeping records on our performances and sincerity.

And there are others from among us who use prayer as a means of personal request. Perhaps we're short of money or possibly having Love problems. We might have a legal problem or need help in making some major decisions concerning any number of variant possibilities.

Many people who consider themselves religious are actually more superstitious than religious, as I see it. They are so thoroughly convinced of their own individual importance in the eyes of the Almighty, that they

---

[13]We are not implying that this was the only impetus for the custom of fasting

think nothing of calling upon god at any hour of the day or night. They will plead with Him to help them solve some personal problems, that they could surely solve for ourselves, if only they would put forth sufficient effort and brain power and faith i.e. Winning Attitude.

I was surprised, while looking at an interview on TV of a rich and influential businessman, when he said in response to a question concerning religion --*"I see my savior every morning in my mirror"*. The statement didn't shock me; it's true and basically accurate. But I was surprised by the source from which those words came. Most people of "Status" don't have the courage to tell the public the Truth!

God demands efficiency

God, whose will is represented by natural law, rewards efficiency; and he condemns inefficiency through a process of natural selection, that is reward (life, health and progeny) to the efficacious, and punishment (death, illness, sterility) to the inefficient. Scientific research confirms that this selective system prevails throughout all of nature, so it must, by that fact alone, be patterned after the mind of the creator god. Nature must reflect the will of its creator, which is god. The natural power of god lies within us, within the fabric of our being – not in artificial images or in imagined counterfeit gods. According to the bible, Jesus stressed the power of faith as the means to god. We've all heard countless laudatory remarks about the amazing powers of faith, human will, love, determination, destiny, concentration, meditation, and prayer – these are all powers bound within the fabric of the human soul and linked somehow with the universal soul, attributes of god imbedded within all of his creation according to some. The objects or icons of our faiths, whether Jesus, Zeus, Allah, Jehovah, Yahweh, the devil, a mountain, a statue, a tree, a river, the sun, the moon, a star, or whatever are only catalyst that tend to spark the fires of faith, and the soul of god that resides within all of us. It is our strong faith and belief, tapping the powers within, that produces so-called miracles, according to some. These so-called miracles of god are miracles produced from powers within, and not from the effete artificial idols and fabricated gods that we bow down to, that are actually the products of our expansive imaginations. Our man-made gods have not the power to help us or hinder us. The only true god is the soul of god that permeates all of his creation, in my humble opinion.

The deluded and less fortunate may, under their various religious banners, seek special favors from god through prayerful supplications, *to alter the natural courses of cause and effect*, so that they are rewarded even when reward is not justly mandated by the *natural laws of cause and effect*. If god answered, or was even capable of answering such supplications, with results that run counter to the natural order of cause and effect, such would upset the harmony and balance of nature, implode the natural order. Hence godly intervention is impossible, if the requested effect runs counter to the natural cause of its generation. Natural order is a series of causes and effects, infinitely interlinked and intertwined. **God cannot alter one natural effect without wreaking devastation upon the whole interlocking system.** No effect happens in isolation but rather is linked interminably through an endless maze of naturally generated consequences. Special favors from god are naturally impossible, because god's systems of natural laws do not allow for exceptions to the natural order. If exceptions were allowed, then nature and universal order would be overturned. The god of monotheism is an imposter, based on this reality alone.

If you're using prayer as means toward inner peace, and connection with our Creator god for inner strength and moral direction, then I think you're on the right track.

But if you think that prayer will produce miracles, or save you from your enemies, or the ravages of a hard life, you are in error! You are wasting precious time that could be more productively spent studying or acting upon your needs and/or problems!

Think not, that I am attempting to denigrate the importance of prayer. I am trying to put prayer in its proper perspective. Through prayer (especially on a regular basis), we remind ourselves of the higher exalted aspects of life. We impress upon our minds the importance of Justice, Truth, Honesty

The Biggest Lie Ever Told, 4th Edition

Pride, Self Respect, Purpose, Consideration, Courage, Fidelity and all the *benevolent attributes* of the god (within and without) to whom we pray!

God doesn't need us to tell him how great he is! *We* need to remind ourselves of the greatness of our creator. *We need not inform god* of our problems. We would be better served to talk to some *living* human being, who's advice we can trust, and who is qualified to assist us in the area of our concern.

Sometimes we may become so confused and uncertain that we can't decide which way to turn. In this state of distress, we may be tempted to fall back in a corner and plead to god for an answer. Every man and woman deserves the right to lick his or her wounds. But this must be, of necessity, a momentary thing. There is an old saying *"god helps those who help themselves"* - truer words were never spoken.

The net result of doing nothing is nothing. Action, on our part, gives god the opportunity to assist us. Action, on our part, gives god the opportunity to guide us.

It needs to be understood that this concept of god, as a potential loving benefactor - from whom favors or mercy could be extracted was born and nurtured by the illusions of primordial man, while in a state of *Not Knowing* how to successfully combat the contentious forces of nature. The greatest and most persistent threat faced by early man, was the potential wrath of the elements, his environment. Therefore man, in his search for god, developed a concept that fitted his need.

Primordial man felt he needed supernatural help or mercy to withstand or overcome the sometimes erratic, vicious forces of nature; which in his underdeveloped intellectual state, he imagined were aimed directly at him. He imagined god to be a loving god (when the environment was pleasant) but sometimes wrathful (in times of a harsh environment).

The Biggest Lie Ever Told, 4th Edition

Thus, primordial man developed the *ritualized* Prayer as a form of communicating his wishes to the almighty master of the elements (his environment) .By means of prayer, man could laud god (flatter him, if you will). prayer was a means of expressing his undying affection for his deity. You are familiar with how obsequious, servile people will heap praise on those whom they fear. Also, through prayer, man can register his request for mercy or help from his deity.

So early mans chief motivation for prayer was his need to develop a channel of communication with the controller of his environment. But look at us now! Should our concept remain unchanged? We now understand our environment. We know that this planet earth is a living pulsing thing, just as we are. Its storms and earthquakes, droughts, scorching heat, freezing cold, tornadoes and the like can quite understandably be compared to our own involuntary reflexes. No amount of prayer can allay our sneezing, coughing, sweating, our chills our belching, our excretory processes, eating, spitting and the rest. These are all part of our life's functions, vital and automatic.

And likewise with our programmed universe, which is made in the image of god - its vibrations and cycles are set and certain. Natural Law (god's law) is the greatest of all truths, it does not waiver.

The Biggest Lie Ever Told, 4th Edition

Other books of similar interest by Malik H Jabbar

The Astrological Foundation Of The Christ Myth, Book One
1-57154 – 010 – 5
$9.95

The Astrological Foundation Of The Christ Myth, Book Two
1 – 57154 – 003 –2
$14.95

The Astrological Foundation Of The Christ Myth, Book Three
1 – 57154 – 004 – 0
$14.95

The Astrological Foundation Of The Christ Myth, Book Four
1 – 57154 – 006 – 7
$14.95

Lifting The Gnostic Veil
1-57154-008-3
$14.95

INDEX

THE BIGGEST LIE EVER TOLD

THE BIGGEST LIE EVER TOLD